WAS
I YOUR
FIRST?

WAS I YOUR FIRST?

Progression of America's First African-American General
Manager for a Major Brand Hotel in USA History

DERK R. MATTOCKS

CITIOFBOOKS, INC.
3736 Eubank NE Suite A1
Albuquerque, NM 87111-3579
www.citiofbooks.com
Hotline: 1 (877) 389-2759
Fax: 1 (505) 930-7244

Ordering Information:

Quantity sales. Special discounts are available on quantity purchases by corporations, associations, and others. For details, contact the publisher at the address above.

Printed in the United States of America.

ISBN-13:   Softcover   978-1-963209-12-9
              eBook   978-1-963209-14-3
              Hardback   978-1-963209-13-6

Library of Congress Control Number: 2023923467

TABLE OF CONTENTS

DEDICATION

I dedicate this book, in loving memory, to my mother, Katie Mae Bell, who set the standard for my focus, my drive, and my ability to manage myself on the path I chose with humility, integrity, generosity, and kindness. And, to my youngest daughter, who too, like her grandmother, is focused, strong, kind, humble, proud, and smart, who inspired me to write this book.

ACKNOWLEDGMENTS

I would like to acknowledge everyone who helped and supported my aspiration, through inspiration and motivation in writing this book, including some adversaries. My story started under the influence of my mother, Katie Mae Bell, who, from before my birth, was my everything. She taught me that God would advance and promote me through his love and appreciation. She would say, "Stay calm and in command of yourself, and you will find out just how easy it is to get along, get things done, and grow." I learned not to accept anything less. My mother's wisdom tips saturated the frontal lobe of my brain.

My daughter, who encouraged me to write this book by asserting that the whole episode of my past was no less than a piece of American history. She wanted me to unfold the story behind being the first African American Hotel General Manager of a white own major brand hotel of my past was no less than a piece of American history. She wanted me to unfold the story behind being the first African American Hotel General Manager of a white own major brand hotel.

The former Ms. Nunez, Aracely, my loving wife of 43 plus years and counting, whose partnership continues to provide me with steadfast support, keeping me balanced and focused while serving as a sounding board of brutal but objective feedback, couched in love and admiration.

Peter Schruender, German-born, senior hotel executive and my mentor, was less influenced by the racial bias directed against Black Americans. Mr. Schruender did not allow his skin color to contaminate his mind with hate, ignorance, and stupidity, as it had done and continues to do to a significant portion of the white population of the U.S.

James L. Wilson, my number-one friend since we met in Chicago, Ill, in 1967. Jim, now Dr. James L. Wilson, DDS, who has practiced dentistry for the last 50 years, and I have sustained the best friend relationship for 55 years. To date, our two-way honest, and objective council to each other during those 55 years has supported and kept each other balanced and focused both personally and professionally during turbulent times.

And, of course, I wish to acknowledge that "significant portion of the white Jim Crow population" on the white side of town who, with their racist and privileged temperament and a disdain for sharing, motivated me to understand that I didn't need their validation. So, my mother's wisdom on self-motivation engaged me to plow ahead, taking on that government-supported open and stealth-structured racist system with an open mind and strategies for my life's success.

Those privileged attitudes and behaviors became my Petri dish, enabling me to study and practice many of my mother's wisdom nuggets, "Stay calm and in command of self, and you will find out just how easy it is to get along, get things done, and grow." I continued striving to live my life, minimizing judgment, anger, hate, and stress, but never foregoing my focus, even though the pain was unbearable at times. Fortunately, during the process, I was able to convert some privileged souls into friends, allies, and at times, accomplices. While many experiences still haunt me and make my stomach churn, my life of hope, happiness, and success has proven worthy of my mother's council.

ABOUT THE AUTHOR

D erk Mattocks, a veteran, corporate executive, government executive, college professor, and entrepreneur, is the author of Was I Your First? The Progression of America's First African American Hotel General Manager of an all-white-owned hotel, on the white side of town, in the United States of America.

Derk started his hotel management career in the late 60s, which lasted for 16 years. He then took on an assignment with a Department of Defense (DOD) agency working for the U.S. Army Community and Family Support Center (USACFSC) for 25 years.

He retired, reinvented himself, and joined Prince George's Community College as an adjunct professor, where he taught for almost a decade. Again, Derk reinvented himself and started his business, Turning Point Coaching, LLC, where he earned certifications in Business, Executive, and Life Coaching, serving the government, non-profits, and the private sector.

Derk's education includes two postgraduate degrees (MBA & MSc. Mgt.) from the University of Maryland University College, College Park, MD, and a Bachelor of Science in Organizational Management from Nyack College, Nyack, New York. He is a United States Army Sustaining Base Leadership Management program (SBLM) graduate from the U.S. Army Management Staff College, Fort Belvoir, VA.

Derk credits his achievements to his ability to stay focused and performance-driven while being strong, kind, humble, and proud, all wrapped in God's blessings.

PREFACE

Derk R. Mattocks was born in the United States, a country plagued with racism. He overcame many challenges throughout his life, facing them head-on rather than running away. His upbringing had some challenges in a society of bigotry. Those challenging experiences were tempered in a local community that showed love through actions. Rest assured, in this community, there were no participation trophies, no accolades for a job left half-completed, and there were consequences for bad behavior.

Derk attributes his accomplishments in life to his mother, schooling in Belgrade Elementary, Silverdale Elementary, Georgetown High, and the community he grew up in. He recalls that all-black sequential and progressive developmental environment for what it was, where people cared about youths, and the youths respected their elders as well. The adults looked out for the youths, helping them when they needed help and leaving them be when they knew the youths needed to figure things out on their own. It was certainly tough, but it built character.

Even though racism, leftover from the immoral stain of slavery, permeated Derk's environment from birth through maturity, he decided that he was not going to let that hold him back. He persevered in his struggles, found mentors, allies, and even accomplices, and excelled in the hospitality industry, where a person of color at top levels of management was previously unimaginable.

Read and find out the life lessons, hard-earned accolades, and principles he employed to push past his comfort zone and win at life.

Chapter 1

Introduction

In an effort to frame and capture the essence and significance of my hotel management career experience and the journey that followed, I needed to gain some insight into other African-American hospitality experiences who had gone on before me.

Insights gained pointed to African-American greats in the hospitality industry during the late 18th century and early 19th century who displayed the highest level of confidence, competence, and courage during turbulent times. Unfortunately, none of these hotel owners were ever allowed to manage an operation in a white-owned hotel establishment. However, they, one after another, were consistently performance-driven and outcome-focused on the colored side of town. So, with the greatest humility and admiration, I pay homage to each of them.

In those times, discrimination and segregation were common and expected throughout the United States of America. Travelers of color were deprived of basic decencies and services. Constantly, Blacks were subjected to the inconvenience and degradation of being denied access to services and businesses. And to make matters worse, the possibility of bigoted violence, including lynching, was left open. The landscape of this country was dotted with 'sundown villages' where the presence of people of color was prohibited after dark. African American car travelers would carry blankets and pillows, extra food, drinks, and gasoline, as well as portable toilets due to the unpredictability of available lodging, food, and fuel.

As an African American, reading about Victor Hugo Green (November 9, 1892 – October 16, 1964) helped me comprehend, frame, and put my 16 years of hotel management experience (1968–1984) into context. Being the first African-American hotel general manager for a global hotel company was part of that experience.

African-American male worker Victor Hugo Green, a travel writer from Harlem, New York City, was best known for his writing and developing skills. The Green Book, a renowned and historic travel guide for African Americans in the United States, was written by him. Blacks required a guidebook to help them integrate black-friendly businesses because of the racist conditions caused by segregation. During the era of Jim Crow legislation and racial segregation in the US, Green astutely examined hotels and restaurants that catered to African Americans. The Green Book, also known as The Negro Motorist Green Book, The Negro Travelers' Green Book, or The Travelers' Green Book, is a travel guide that was published in the United States between the years of 1936 and 1967 while legal segregation was still in effect. It listed companies that welcomed African Americans as clients. Before the Civil Rights Act of 1964, the Green Book provided a comprehensive catalog of establishments required to ensure that African Americans could travel comfortably and safely. These establishments ranged from restaurants and hotels to beauty parlors and pharmacies. I, a black man, was hired into an exclusively white-owned hospitality (hotel) management industry only four years later, in 1968, shattering decades of racial barriers supported by the government, society, and governmental sanctions.

I was born in mid-1945, amid the baby boomer generation. Consequently, I was born, reared, educated, and employed during the baby boomer era, marked by revolutionary, collectivist, and ideological tendencies. Whether true or not, I would assert that these foundational characteristics allowed me to be objective, performance-driven, and outcome-oriented. Adapting to the succeeding generations (such as GEN X, GEN Y, and GEN Z) was not challenging. I accepted my faults, ventured outside my comfort zone, and devised strategies for success. I easily identified the connections between concepts, evaluated the significance and applicability of additions, and approached problems consistently and methodically. To achieve this, I maintained an open mind and a growth mindset. Regardless of the difficulty, reinventing myself and adapting to unfamiliar environments came naturally to me. And I witnessed the epitome of hate with the killing of John F. Kennedy, our 35th President of the United States (1961–1963) in 1963.

Martin Luther King, Jr., an American Baptist minister and activist, was one of the most well-known figures in America from 1955 until his assignation, April 4, 1968, in Memphis Tennessee).

Stokely Carmichael, also known as Kwame Ture (June 29, 1941– November 15, 1998), was a well-known American figure active in the civil rights movement and the global Pan-African movement from 1955 until 1998.

I grew up in an environment where I was familiar with these important figures. Additionally, being an avid reader, I was fortunate to gain much insight, from an early age, into my ancestors' contributions to society. My ancestors' history, both oral and written, fueled my drive, enabling me to maintain my focus with purpose. To that end, I have always been performance-driven and outcome-focused to live up to what I believed to be my ancestors' expectations. That is my way of contributing to the preparation that my lineage who follows is positioned to be even better than my own.

My daughter, who wrote the first draft version of this book, is a millennial, and millennials, too, have had their share of turbulence, coming of age. That turbulence includes but is not limited to 9/11, the 2008 recession, Barack Obama as the First Black President, the COVID-19 Pandemic, Donald Trump as the first Twice Impeached President within four years, and The January 6 insurrection in our government, and Donald Trump as the first ex-president to be indited, leaving a trail of division and political discourse. History speaks volumes about who suffered the consequences when the "significant portion of the white population," with their disdain for sharing America, gained power.

America suffers...

The many interviews my daughter did with me gave me more insight into myself. But more than that was the insight that her interviewing me gave me into her mindset. And that insight of my daughter is forever priceless. I am so proud of what I saw.

She spoke proudly, saying, "Because of people like my parents and my ancestors, I can go out in public and live my life unapologetically with the confidence, competence, and courage that represents me."

She made it clear that had it not been for those who stood up when enough was enough, her life would have been very different today.

She proudly asserted, "Dad, you are one of those people who broke through the prejudices and persevered through so many barriers, always striving to excel and doing so against all odds. I am so proud of you. And yes, your story must be told, but told by you in your own words."

What a great return on investment...A mind of enlightenment; a mind of confidence; a mind of competence, and a mind of courage...

During my extensive reading, I came across a piece by an unidentified author that motivated and supported my deepest commitment by highlighting how black people, my progenitors (DNA), were forcibly brought to North America. Although I was born in this country, my DNA was carried here in chains. The article spoke to me personally when it stated that my people were brought here against their will by transportation conditions that were abhorrent, devoid of human dignity, and even more lethal, and yet my DNA remained steadfast.

While they did not speak the new world's language, my DNA prevailed. Surviving members of my ancestry were tortured, raped, and forced to work long hours without compensation, all while significantly contributing to this land. Others, including women, children, and men, who shared my DNA were sold off like cattle, de-programmed, turned against each other, and prevented from basic literacy such as learning to read and write.

Even when my ancestors earned the right, donned military uniforms, became soldiers and officers, and fought overseas under the flag of the United States of America in defense of this land, they did not have a place to return to where they were accepted and honored for their valorous service. Many of my people suffered injuries, while others made the supreme sacrifice. Nonetheless, those who were able to return home with my DNA were attacked, beaten, and hanged by the white privileged, and there is still no justice for their souls to this day.

My DNA persisted despite everything. Developing self-care practices, they persisted and eventually flourished without white privilege validation, as I believe that is what God intended. My mother had predicted my fate. God did advance, promote, and keep me. My success was more of an inevitability than a choice because it was ingrained in my mentality as a fact of life. As a result, I was naturally confident. After all, my people could face the hatred and violence that the government had authorized that was permeating them from all sides.

They were intensely committed to not just surviving but succeeding. I, an offspring, had no choice but to respect their sacrifices, understanding that I, Derk R. Mattocks was a return on their investment. I felt obligated to ensure that my ancestors' investment was profitable. I needed a strategy to deal with, control, and navigate that 'significant percentage of the privileged white population' and their Jim Crow and government-supported structural oppression. That plan was my ability to comprehend and love myself fully. As far as I'm concerned, no one else can love me the way I do.

It also included other tools to combat the perspective that a 'significant portion of the Jim Crow population' would obstruct my progress, including my capacity to understand connections between ideas and recognize, build, and appraise arguments. The numerous obstacles put up to tripped me proved challenging but not too difficult for my reasoning strategy, open-mindedness, analysis, and logic to dismantle.

My mother's advice to "Stay calm and in command of yourself, and you will find out just how simple it is to get along, get things done, and grow" was spot on.

My self-management strategy incorporated all my mother's advice. One is, silencing the negative voice in my head. Knowing that keeping my private conversations with my Lord would guide me to my supercomputer (brain), a brilliant bit of His work, making it capable for me to do a tremendous amount of data processing. My stored memories took me to experiences I had gone through, read, or heard about.

Sometimes they were easy to access, while at other times, it took some work to open certain mental file drawers in my brain. Not all the memories were good when it came to how Blacks were treated. To silence that negative voice in my head, I started practicing the science of neuro-linguistic programming (NLP), which helped me with changing what my memory meant to me.

Neuro-linguistic programming helped enhance and reinforce my never-give-up attitude. I learned to change how I talk to myself. When I changed how I talked to myself, I became unstoppable, as the majority, if not all the negative issues discussed in my mind started to dissolve. Trust me. It was an amazing feeling as my confidence elevated in all that I did. I pushed my can-do attitude severalfold by eliminating negative words from my vocabulary and replacing them with positive thoughts. Discipline was in my hands. So, I made a choice.

Being an avid reader and listener, not all of my recollections of how Black people were treated were positive. The process of NLP helped me change what my memory meant to me by helping me to quiet that critical voice in my mind. Neuro-linguistic programming has improved my 'never give up' mindset. I've learned to modify the way I speak to myself. I became unstoppable once I altered how I spoke to myself because most—if not all—of the negative things I had been talking about began to go away.

Believe me. It was a wonderful sensation as my self-confidence increased in everything I did by removing negative words from my vocabulary and substituting them with positive thoughts. I multiplied the impact of my optimistic outlook. I had control over discipline, and the same was the case with my decisions.

The second most valuable piece of advice was associating pain with moving outside my comfort zone for the dream I was seeking. Yes, 'going for it all.' The agony that I could control, I controlled. The pain that I could tolerate, I tolerated it. I am familiar with both physical and mental suffering. Recovering from my automobile accident, I renamed the mental anguish associated with the prospect of never walking again so that I could easily adopt a 'never give up' attitude. I learned to associate mental anguish with ending procrastination and distraction while adopting a patient, persistent, and tenacious mindset.

I adopted the attitude of 'It Ain't Nothing to It But To Do It.' And I was proven right, again and again.

Concentrating on the delight of my voyage or rather the simple pleasure of my journey motivated me to hold on to my patient, persistent, and tenacious attitude. The belief that most, if not all, things should be simple was one of the greatest obstacles I encountered in adopting such an outlook. I never imagined that a 'significant portion of the ardent Jim Crow population' would facilitate my entry, employment, and advancement in the hospitality industry. However, I knew the answer had more to do with me than with that Jim Crow cohort. I was mentally prepared for the roadblocks continually being placed in my path.

I have always believed this was my turn and moment to deserve it all, as I am the result of my ancestors' sacrifices. I considered any obstacles that caused me physical, mental, or emotional pain to be the sole indicators that I was alive. I can now acknowledge without remorse that those obstacles made me stronger, enhancing the satisfaction of my successes. Now, when I look back, I can see how I overcame those obstacles. I am aware that nothing could have prevented me from proceeding. I now experience immense joy and am always up for a new challenge.

Recognizing patience, persistence, and perseverance as important and influential behaviors were insightful. Together, they fueled the pursuit of my professional and personal objectives. I created a plan of action and milestones (POAM), worked on the process, and allotted the necessary time to achieve the desired results. Having to navigate that 'significant segment of the adamant Jim Crow population' taught me the value of patience, persistence, and perseverance. Similarly, my ability to intertwine those qualities in my plan of action and milestone enabled me to remain firm on my course despite opposition enacted by a 'significant portion of the diehard Jim Crow population.' Their white privilege mentality and disdain for sharing inspired me to demonstrate that I did not require their approval.

When it comes to how that population treated blacks, the problems we face today are nothing new. So much of the long list of atrocities committed against my ancestors does not appear in any history book. Everything is an incomplete representation of the truth, from the masked references in textbooks to the disparaging condition we were kept in. However, the prejudice, hate, and malice held by people who wrote our history were more horrendous than one can ever imagine. With that in mind, my daughter, let me know, in no uncertain terms, the urgency for me to write my own American story.

My "baby boomer" generational experience began in 1945 in Belgrade, North Carolina, a small black community located 350 miles south and southeast of Washington, D.C. After several years, I began my formal education. I say formal education because my informal village education began before I could walk. My formal education began in a three-room, one-story building in my neighborhood that offered first (1st) through seventh (7th) grades. The first, second, and third classes were taught in one classroom, the fourth and fifth grades in another, and the sixth and seventh grades in the third. Despite multiple grade levels in the same classroom, I cannot recall a single instance of significant conflict between the students. This three-room schoolhouse, where I learned so much about people, places, and things, which was expanded and reinforced as I progressed through elementary and secondary school, planted the seed for my desire to travel the world.

During my first twelve years (elementary through high school), the only instructors (formal and informal) I ever learned from were black. And yes, I received an education that included challenges, critical thinking, and the basics of self-discovery and sustainability. The overall development program prepared and empowered me intellectually, emotionally, socially, and with endurance to compete with the best of the best by instilling in me a solid foundation of confidence, competence, and fortitude.

My entry into college was the first time I had a white instructor. And regardless, it did not matter to me. My only objective was to gain knowledge from professors, other students, and anyone else who crossed my path with something to impart.

Returning and reflecting on my elementary schooling in that three-room schoolhouse, in addition to learning about people, places, and objects, I was also taught there to respect and appreciate others. I was always instructed to maintain a respectful and dignified demeanor.

I credit my parents, the community of Belgrade, and my teachers for providing me with a firm foundation for developing a performance-driven and outcome-focused mindset.

After completing third grade, I departed the three-room schoolhouse. My fellow students and I were transported by bus to a newly constructed brick elementary school in Silverdale, North Carolina, approximately 15 miles away. There, I was enlightened and created uplifting memories as a consequence of enlightening experiences. I participated in team sports throughout middle school.

After completing Silverdale Elementary School, I attended Georgetown High School. Georgetown High was located in Jacksonville, North Carolina. Again, we were transported approximately 15 miles to Georgetown High School, where I graduated four years later in 1963. While at Georgetown High, in addition to academics, I was anxious and encouraged to broaden my issues. The insights I acquired from engaging topics were always enlightening. These points of interest were frequently outside my comfort zone, challenging, enchanting, and rewarding. There, I developed my self-discipline while learning to question the status quo.

While at Georgetown High, the movement of pressing for African Americans' civil rights was on the rise. The white privileged segment of American society, enveloped in Jim Crow practices and supported by the government, made it extremely difficult for African Americans to obtain their rights (liberty and justice). Still, we fought relentlessly but in a nonviolent manner.

When I was in the fourth grade at Silverdale Elementary School, I read and heard a lot about Dr. Martin Luther King, Jr., when on December 1, 1955, in Montgomery, Alabama, police officers arrested Mrs. Rosa Parks for 'unrepentantly' refusing to give up her bus seat to a white male. There was speculation that Dr. Martin Luther King, Jr. would come to Mrs. Parks' defense. That was when I sought to observe and comprehend the true meaning of challenging the status quo. Dr. Martin Luther King, Jr. was known for simultaneously comforting the disturbed and disturbing the comfortable.

I learned early that challenging the status quo generates disruption. Adam Mattocks, my first cousin and 12 years my senior, as a young man, was prominent in the Civil Rights movement. During my elementary and secondary school years, Adam was my influence and introduced me to and opened my eyes to this turbulence, which included the following:

Grade and Elementary School

1954 - May 17, The Supreme Court of the United States unanimously ruled that racial segregation in public schools is unconstitutional in Brown v. Board of Education.

1955 - December 1, Mrs. Rosa Parks, a 42-year-old Montgomery seamstress, was arrested when she refused to give up her bus seat to a white man.

December 5, The first day of the Montgomery bus boycott.

December 10, The Montgomery Bus Company suspended service in Black Americans' neighborhoods.

1956 - January 30, A bomb was thrown onto the porch of Dr. King's Montgomery home.

February 2, A suit was filed in Federal District courts asking that Montgomery's travel segregation laws be declared unconstitutional.

February 21, Dr. King was indicted for the Montgomery bus boycott as a party to a conspiracy to hinder business without "just or legal cause."

June 4, The United States District Court ruled that segregation on city bus lines was unconstitutional.

June 27, Dr. King Spoke at the National Association for the Advancement of Color People (NAACP) convention in San Francisco.

August 10, Dr. King Spoke at the committee of the Democratic Party in Chicago.

October 30, The Mayor of Montgomery, Alabama, sought legal action to stop the operation of carpools and transportation systems growing out of the Montgomery boycott.

November 13, The United States Supreme Court affirmed the decision of the three-judge district court in declaring unconstitutional Alabama's state and local laws requiring segregation on buses.

December 20, Federal injunctions prohibiting bus segregation were served on city and bus company officials in Montgomery and state officials.

December 21, Montgomery buses were integrated.

1957 - January 10-11, The Southern Christian Leadership Conference (SCLC) was formed at Ebenezer Baptist Church, Atlanta. Dr. King was elected President.

February 18, Time magazine puts Dr. King on its cover.

May 17, Dr. King delivered a speech for the Prayer Pilgrimage for Freedom celebrating the 3rd anniversary of the Supreme Court's desegregation decision entitled "Give us the Ballot," at the Lincoln Memorial, Washington, DC.

June 13, Dr. King had a conference with the Vice President of the United States, Richard Nixon.

September 1957, When Governor Faubus ordered the Arkansas National Guard to surround Central High School to keep the nine black students from entering the school, President Eisenhower ordered the 101st Airborne Division into Little Rock to safeguard the nine black kids and that the rulings of the Supreme Court were upheld.

September 9, the first Civil Rights Act since Reconstruction, was passed by Congress. Creating the Civil Rights Commission and the Civil Rights Division of the Department of Justice.

1958 - June 23, Dr. King, Roy Wilkin of the NAACP, A. Phillip Randolph, and Lester Granger met with President Eisenhower.

September 3, Dr. King was arrested on a charge of loitering (later changed to failure to obey orders of an officer) in the vicinity of Montgomery recorder's court and released on a $100 bond.

September 4, Dr. King was convicted after pleading not guilty to a charge of failure to obey an officer; the fine was paid almost immediately, over Dr. King's objection, by Montgomery Police Commissioner Clyde C. Sellers.

September 20, Dr. King was stabbed in the chest by Mrs. Izola Curry, 42, who was subsequently alleged to be mentally deranged. The stabbing occurred in the heart of Harlem while Dr. King was autographing his recently published book. Dr. King's condition was said to be severe but not critical.

1959 - January 30, Dr. King met with the Detroit United Auto Workers Union leader.

February 3, Dr. King and his wife spent a month in India studying.

March 10, Gandhi's techniques of nonviolence as a guest of Prime Minister Nehru.

Rest assured, young minds develop and mature fast with access to radio and nurtured by concerned parents, caring teachers and a close nit community.

High School

1960 - February 1 Students in Greensboro, North Carolina, held a lunch counter sit-in to desegregate eating facilities.

April 15 The Student Nonviolent Coordinating Committee (SNCC) was founded to temporarily coordinate student protests at Shaw University, Raleigh, North Carolina. (It was to become a permanent organization in October 1960).

1961 - May 4 The first group of Freedom Riders, intent on integrating interstate buses, left Washington, DC, by Greyhound bus. The group, organized by the Congress for Racial Equality (CORE), left shortly after the Supreme Court outlawed segregation in interstate transportation terminals. The bus was burned outside of Anniston, Alabama, on May 14. A mob beat the Riders upon their arrival in Birmingham. The Riders were arrested in Jackson, Mississippi, and spent 40 to 60 days in Parchman Penitentiary.

1962 - September 20, James Meredith made his first attempt to enroll at the University of Mississippi. He was enrolled by Supreme Court Order and escorted onto the Oxford, Mississippi, campus by U.S. Marshalls on October 1.

Mar-Apr

Sit-in demonstrations were held in Birmingham to protest the segregation of eating facilities.

May 3-5, Eugene ("Bull") Connor, director of public safety of Birmingham, orders the use of police dogs and fire hoses upon the marching protesters (young adults and children).

May 20, The United States Supreme Court ruled Birmingham's segregation ordinance unconstitutional.

1963 - February 1, Governor George C. Wallace tried to stop the court-ordered integration of the University of Alabama by "standing in the schoolhouse door" and personally refusing entrance to black students and Justice Department officials. President John F. Kennedy then federalized the Alabama National Guard, and Governor Wallace removed himself from blocking the entrance of the Negro Students.

August 28, The March on Washington, the first integrated protest march for jobs and freedom, was held in Washington, DC.

Sept 2-10, Governor Wallace ordered the Alabama State Troopers to stop the court-ordered integration of Alabama's elementary and high schools until a court injunction from doing so enjoins him. By September 10, specific schools are integrated by court order.

On November 22, President Kennedy was assassinated in Dallas, Texas.

College

1964 – Summer, The Council of Federated Organizations initiated the Mississippi Summer Project, a voter registration drive organized and run by black and white students.

June 21, three civil rights workers -James Chaney (black), Andrew Goodman, and Michael Schwerner (white) were reported missing after a short trip to Philadelphia, Mississippi.

Jul 18-23, Riots occurred in Harlem; one black man was killed.

August 1964 – Riots occurred in New Jersey, Illinois, and Pennsylvania.

August 4, the bodies of civil rights workers James Chaney (Black), Andrew Goodman, and Michael Schwerner (both white) were discovered by FBI agents buried near the town of Philadelphia, Mississippi. Neshoba County Sheriff Rainey and his deputy, Cecil Price, were allegedly implicated in the murders.

1965 - February 21, Malcolm X, leader of the Organization of Afro-American Unity and former Black Muslim leader, was murdered allegedly by blacks in New York City.

March 7, A group of marching demonstrators (from SNCC and SCLC) led by SCLC's Hosea Williams were beaten while attempting to march across the Edmund Pettus Bridge on their planned march to Montgomery, Alabama, from Selma, Alabama, by state highway patrolmen under the direction of Al Lingo and sheriff's deputies under the leadership of Jim Clark. An order by Governor Wallace had prohibited the march.

March 9, Unitarian minister James Reeb was beaten by four white segregationists in Selma and died two days later.

March 15, President Johnson addressed the nation and Congress. He described the Voting Rights Bill he will submit to Congress in two days and used the slogan of the civil rights movement, "We shall overcome."

March 16, Black and white demonstrators were beaten by sheriff deputies and police on horseback in Montgomery.

Mar 21-25, over 3,000 protest marchers left Selma to march to Montgomery, protected by federal troops. They were joined along the way by a total of 25,000 marchers. Upon reaching the capitol building, they heard an address by Dr. King.

March 25, Mrs. Viola Liuzzo, wife of a Detroit Teamsters Union business agent, was shot and killed while driving a carload of marchers back to Selma.

Aug-Dec, In Alabama, SCLC spearheads voter registration campaigns in Greene, Wilcox, Eutaw Counties, Montgomery, and Birmingham. President Johnson signed August 6 the 1965 Voting Rights Act.

Aug 11-16, In Watts, the black ghetto of Los Angeles, riots left 35 dead, of whom 28 were black.

1966 - March 25, The U.S. Supreme Court ruled any poll tax unconstitutional. Spring The Alabama primary was held, the first time since Reconstruction that blacks have voted in any number.

June 6, Stokely Carmichael and Willie Ricks (SNCC) used the slogan "Black Power" in public for the first time before reporters in Greenwood, Mississippi.

September – SCLC launched a project to integrate schools in Grenada, Mississippi. Fall SCLC initiated the Alabama Citizen Education Project in Wilcox County.

1967 - March 12, Alabama was ordered to desegregate all public schools.

May 10 -11, One black student was killed in rioting on the campus of all Negro Jackson State College, Jackson, Mississippi.

July 6, The Justice Department reported that more than 50 percent of all eligible black voters were registered in Mississippi, Georgia, Alabama, Louisiana, and South Carolina.

Jul 12-17, twenty-three people died, and 725 were injured in riots in Newark, New Jersey.

Jul 23-30, forty-three people, 324, were injured in Detroit riots, the worst of the century.

1968 - February 12 Sanitation workers strike in Memphis, Tennessee.

Just a little background on Adam C. Mattocks, who influenced my focus on higher education:

Adam Mattocks was a man of immense character and fortitude. He served from 1957 to 1964, flying B-52s bombers and other planes. Adam was committed to civil rights and was devoted to making the world better for everyone around him. His humility and selflessness were evident in his interactions with his family, friends, colleagues, and community.

Adam and I are first cousins and grew up as brothers. Adam, twelve years my senior, was the first member of the Mattocks family to attend and graduate from college (A&T University). He was a mentor, a motivator, a source of new inspiration, and a significant influence on the path I chose to pursue. He was an example for the entire community and society.

Adam, an individual with multiple missions, answered the call to serve by learning and flying multiple style plans and fighting for civil rights. When I was asked to deliver the eulogy at Adam's funeral, my reflections on his life revealed how instrumental he was in molding my life.

Adam's numerous accomplishments, and there were many, were motivated by his desire to serve others. Adam served as a pilot in the United States Air Force from 1 957 to 1964 after graduating from A&T University. He specialized in flying aircraft such as the Lockheed T-33 Shooting Star Jet-Powered Trainer Aircraft, the F-86, a transonic jet fighter aircraft, and the Boeing B-52 Stratofortress long-range, subsonic, jet-powered strategic bomber.

In 1961, during the Cold War, 1st Lt. Mattocks and nine crew members embarked on a 24-hour mission carrying two Hydrogen Bombs that were more potent than the bombs that destroyed Hiroshima. They collided in Goldsboro, North Carolina. This mission and its results are described in 'The Goldsboro Broken Arrow.'

Following his return to civilian life, Adam:

- Fought for Black Pilots seeking pilot positions with commercial airlines while fighting racial discrimination.

- Became the first Black Department Head as Director of the Onslow County Fund for the Underprivileged and War on Poverty.

- Started Head-start in Onslow County, N.C.

- Implemented the first Community Action Program in neighborhoods, setting up community centers to improve neighborhoods by conducting revitalization efforts and social justice programs.

- Became the first Black member of the Economic Improvement Board, which worked with County officials in establishing the Albert J. Ellis Airport.

- Became President of the Onslow County Chapter of the NAACP, where he served for 25 years.

- Assisted in diversifying schools with teachers, students of color, and other institutions such as banks.

- Instrumental in growing the KUUMBA Festival, where the world meets to celebrate BLACK ART, CULTURE & HERITAGE) by inviting national entertainment and showcasing local artists.

Adam was a member of my family, a mentor, and a close friend, and I consulted with him on various issues, such as comprehending the social justice environment and the progress made due to Dr. King's efforts to soothe the disturbed and disturb the comfortable.

During my high school graduation from Georgetown, there was much discussion about integrating public institutions. Every school I attended before that time was segregated by color. The 1964 Civil Rights Act paved the way for school integration in my region, despite the opposition of many whites.

A couple of years after I graduated from high school, my alma mater, Georgetown High, suffered a terrible calamity when it was bombed and burned several hours before the commencement ceremonies. Integration of the institution was under consideration. The American underbelly of society was reemerging and, in my opinion, contributing to the destabilization of society as it reared its hideous head. I could only conclude that this American underbelly viewed continued segregation as essential to their survival. The fabric of bigotry continues to permeate our society today. And this animosity appears to be more blatant than it was when I was younger. Nevertheless, prejudice remains profoundly ingrained in the fabric of our society.

Our society suffered a tremendous loss on the day that Georgetown High School was blasted and destroyed. The brilliant young intellectuals, who would become the pioneers of tomorrow, were left with mental and emotional trauma. Despite adversity, these were good children who had graduated from high school and merely desired to do well and continue with their lives.

At the time of composing this book, it has been 58 years since Georgetown High School closed its doors for good. However, the students who attended the school before the tragic event continue to reunite to remember the happy times we shared and keep the school's legacy alive. Every two years since 1981, the Georgetown High School National Alumni Association has held a reunion. My class, GHS Class of 1963, will hold our 60th anniversary this year, June 28-29, 2023, of which I am honored to have been selected as keynote speaker.

The racial and anti-Semitic violence that devastated Georgetown High, my alma mater, is just one of the catastrophes that have touched many lives, including mine.

History will always speak to the uniqueness of Georgetown High School and its significance as a part of American history in its own right. As Joseph Parsons Brown has documented, Georgetown High was one of a kind.

GEORGETOWN HIGH: As asserted by Joseph Parsons Brown in his book "The Commonwealth of Onslow - A History", published by The Owen G. Dunn Company, New Bern, N. C., J. Y. Joyner Library, East Carolina University, Georgetown High, has an unusual but interesting history. He points to several characteristics that support his assertion; for example, The school was established in 1890 by the Trent River- Oakey Grove Missionary Baptist Association in Pollocksville, N.C., of Jones County; Ministers and Trustees at the beginning included S. M. Scott, C. S. Scott, Senus Hill, W. H. Haddock, J. E. Everette, W. H. Moore, and A. J. Jones; with its purpose to train the youth of the church. Ten years later in the year 1900, the school was transferred to Georgetown and added a dormitory to accommodate students who lived too far from home to rely on the poor transportation available to them in those days.

Joseph Parsons Brown noted that sponsors who contributed to Georgetown High support during those early years included the Trent River Association, the school faculty, Dr. Sharp, and Parent-Teacher Association chapters at Jacksonville, N.C., and Sneads Ferry, N.C. Marshal Chapel and Richlands, N.C. And, in many cases, the teachers contributed their last month's check to meet expenses. He points out that the first principal seems to have been Professor W. H. Hill who was followed by H. J. Hyman and W. Parker, respectively.

Joseph Parsons Brown pointed out that as time went on, the State took over the payment of the Principal's salary and assumed more and more of the control and expense of operating the school.

He noted that the first trucks, operated by the Association, traveled from Sneads Ferry, Richlands, and Piney Green, but the multiplicity of enrollment made the Association's effort seem ineffective.

Joseph Parsons Brown points out that when the State took over the schools in 1933, it became a new era for Georgetown. That new era for Georgetown included a proposal to build a brick building, and that colored citizens would provide several thousand bricks as their contribution to the effort. He asserts that funds were secured as a Federal project during the depression in the early thirties resulting in the first unit of the modern brick structure now in use. Buses were routed throughout the County and a first-class Negro High School was in the making. He notes that credit for much of the early progress at Georgetown should be given to the Reverend J. T. Kerr, who came into the County in 1912 and concentrated his effort on improving the schools of his race and establishing a church in the town of Jacksonville, N.C. (The First Baptist Church now on Court Street.). The city would later name a street in his honor. Reverend J. T. Kerr died in 1932. He was succeeded as Principal by Professor Clifton McLendon and subsequently by Principal, J. W. Broadhurst.

Joseph Parsons Brown noted that in the early 50's the county voted a $1,100,000.00 bond issue plus money allocated for federally connected children by the United States Government, with Georgetown being granted $375,000.00 of this money for capital improvement, which more than doubled the capacity of the school, plus modern equipment and a modern gymnasium equaling the best in the County. Joseph Parsons Brown went on to point out that the school has a good band, an excellent recreation program, and a splendid agricultural course.

Joseph Parsons Brown noted that in 1958 Georgetown High became a fully accredited member of the Southern Association of Colleges and Secondary Schools, which was an exceptional achievement. Professor J. W. Broadhurst, who was Principal since 1937, is acknowledged as being an excellent administrator. Noting that under his supervision the school has made outstanding progress. And that Professor J. W. Broadhurst is active in church and welfare work, and constantly promoting and uplifting his community, both educationally and morally.

Joseph Parsons Brown points to 1959-1960 as growth years with enrollment exceeding 1500 students, with a corps of 49 teachers. The steady growth in enrollment over the years supports the fact that more classrooms will be needed soon, with more teachers to support them. As per Joseph Parsons Brown, the problem is a continuing one. (Thanks to Elora Leven, Annie Washington, and Mrs. J. W. Broadhurst.)

Studying under the umbrella of Georgetown I learned, as Winston Churchill would say, "You will never reach your destination if you stop and throw stones at every dog that barks." So, I refuse to allow hatred and rage to control my existence. Even though it was distressing at times, I refused to let it distract me. Numerous years have passed, and I continue to endure a multitude of bigoted and hateful encounters. Still, treating others with disdain or wrath is not my strong suit. I have learned to be resilient without being impolite.

Similarly, I've learned to be kind without being fragile and contrite without being cowardly. And I am proud that my discipline governs my desire to treat everyone with decency and courtesy. Therefore, I've learned not to settle for less.

Respect and decency are the pillars upon which I've constructed my personality. The respect I show to those who do not merit it reflects more on my character than on theirs. Because of racism, I have effectively navigated some of the most difficult situations and times that any man, black or white, should have to endure.

I have traveled approximately twenty times throughout the Pacific Rim, the Middle East, Europe, portions of Africa, Central and South America, and the United States. I have encountered numerous individuals of all races, creeds, colors, and ethnicities throughout my life. As long as it was legal, moral, and ethical, I have done a little bit of everything, whether in an official or personal capacity. I am, therefore, proud to be the individual I am, who also happens to be black.

My ancestry links me to the masonry and construction trades. My ancestors were also farmers, contractors, and builders of residences and commercial structures. Then came me. From a very young age, I knew that neither cultivation nor construction would be on my résumé. The construction industry was an excellent way for blacks to make decent money, but I had no interest in it. I felt in no way that it was beneath me! I never intended to spend eight to ten hours a day laying masonry and blocks. Family and friends openly said masonry and farming were not my cup of tea. I believed them and pursued other directions.

I broke stereotypes by becoming the first African-American general manager of a white-owned major brand hotel. This opportunity presented itself only three years after the 1965 signature of the Voting Rights Act and one year after the bombing and burning of my high school in 1966.

Real opportunities in upper-level management were considered to be reserved for whites at the time, so blacks could not aspire to obtain positions in hospitality management at the highest levels. During that era, blacks had no chance of becoming anything other than a bellhop, housekeeper, or cook at a prominent hotel. However, I had no intention of allowing my race to hinder my upward mobility.

Early on, I realized that choosing the correct path in life is an art. Key pillars of my path to success were cultivating the right mindset, developing the right skill set, and accumulating the right toolbox. All consisted of sincerity, morality, and ethics, augmented with wit and fortitude cloaked in respect and dignity. Few things can be compared to living in such a fashion. It is a choice to live a moral and upright existence. I chose this path when I was on the cusp of maturity, surrounded by family members who provided me with stability. Respect is mutually beneficial. Early on, I realized that you receive what you give. Although this may sound trite, I cannot think of a better way to say it.

I believe that a person's character is most tested during times of great adversity. I sought employment shortly after graduating from high school and was employed by the Marine Corps, Special Services at Camp Lejeune, North Carolina. However, after working there for several months, I was involved in a head-on collision with a drunk motorist. As a passenger seated in the front seat, the engine of the vehicle wound up resting in my lap. The intoxicated driver and his passenger died on site.

I cannot recall anything about the car catastrophe to this day. In my late teens, I sustained a fractured back, a fractured femur, a fractured skull, and a fractured jaw.

My family and physicians informed me that it was unlikely that I would ever walk again. I am a man who fears God. And while I respected the physician's professional opinions, I submitted my challenge to God. My mother had previously informed me that God would advance, promote, and preserve me. Therefore, I knew in my heart that the doctors' decision would not be conclusive.

My injuries necessitated the placement of a 14-inch titanium rod in the fractured bone of my left quadriceps, which occurred during the accident. This titanium rod remains in my femur to this day.

The one thing that irritated me the most was hearing physicians discussing how unlikely it was that I would ever walk again. At that moment, I resorted to the only power I knew I could depend on my Lord and Redeemer. I continued to pray to my God, as I always had, for the fortitude to overcome my physical, mental, and emotional wounds. My petitions were answered when, after months of difficult rehabilitation work, I was not only walking but also running, jumping, and playing sports.

During those challenging times, the words of a family friend, Ms. Lorrain Ellis, were one of my greatest sources of inspiration, saying: "If you take one step, He will take two for you."

I took these words literally and believed, "If I took one step, my Lord would assist me to take the next two."

I took a few steps, followed by several more until I stopped counting. Even though I could not locate 'if you take one step, He will take two' in the Bible, I felt that my life had been a series of successful steps that have carried me along the path to success in every objective and endeavor I have ever set. Whether it pertained to my spirituality, career, or simply assisting those in need, I have always achieved the goals I set for myself.

A few months after my recovery, I received my conscription notice from the Army. I answered the summons with interest and pride. I was in the midst of basic training at Fort Bragg, North Carolina, and was mentally prepared for Phase II, or AIT, eager to qualify for the U.S. Army Airborne School at Fort Benning, Georgia. However, that was not in the cards. I unwisely participated in a community baseball pick-up game while on a weekend pass and severely injured my left ankle.

My injured ankle was on the same leg that was injured in the auto accident. The ankle injury resulted in a 45-day hospitalization at Fort Bragg's Womack Army Hospital, followed by an honorable discharge for physical disability.

I had my usual private conversation with the Lord and felt compelled to move on, let the decision stand, and refocus my commitment. I returned home after recovering from the ankle injury, departing Womack Army Hospital, and receiving my discharge. After completing a couple of correspondence courses, the desire to move on grew so strong that I was home for less than a couple of months before repacking and leaving for Chicago, Illinois, to pursue my ambition of earning a civil engineering degree.

Before the accident, I had been accepted into several institutions, including Chicago Tech, which was my top choice. I was readmitted to the university and completed three semesters. Dissatisfied with an unpleasant experience during my fourth semester at Chicago Tech, I dropped out, changed my major, and decided to work full-time for a while.

The move and my change in focus led to me becoming the first African-American General Manager of a hotel, food and beverage, and entertainment operations for a white-owned international brand hotel chain in the history of the United States due to a strong desire to maintain balance, refocus, reinvent myself, and move on. I operated hotels on the white side of town for 12 of my 16 years in the hospitality industry. I earned two postgraduate degrees (MBA and MSc. Mgt) from the Graduate School of Management & Technology, University of Maryland; a Bachelor of Science in Organizational Management from Nyack College, New York; and I am a graduate of the U.S. Army's Installation Management and Leadership program from the Army Management Staff College (AMSC), Fort Belvoir, VA.

CHAPTER 2

Impressionable Years

Civil Rights and the fight for social justice on behalf of African Americans occupied my thoughts from elementary school through high school. Dr. Martin Luther King Jr. brought the struggle for civil rights into our homes, classrooms, and living spaces. My cousin Adam Mattocks bolstered and supported Dr. King's message by spreading it throughout the neighborhood.

The civil rights movement and the struggle for social justice for Black Americans during the 1950s and 1960s mirrored my education during grade school through college.

I learned extensively about government and Christian-supported slave owners who brought my ancestors aboard slave ships on the voyage to the New World, subjecting my ancestors (its "cargo") to unimaginable horror.

However, it appears that the owners were unaware of the possibility that we would one day change the situation and become equals. It appears that the abhorrent 'significant portion of the white population' lacked the foresight to realize that putting the genie back in the bottle would be impossible for their descendants. In the end, while still privileged, they despise having to share.

My femur was fractured in an automobile accident, leaving me with the very real possibility that I would never walk again. In essence, each physician I consulted informed me that there was little to no chance I could ever stand ordinarily again. In other words, walking with a hindrance or worse is inevitable. Even though the response devastated me, I would not accept their diagnosis as a remedy. I was not born a quitter. I continued to practice what I had preached to others confidently. I am confident that anyone can surmount life's challenges if they have a strong enough faith in God, exercise self-control, and are sufficiently committed to their desired outcome. To put it simply, I was not a quitter.

The phrase I lived by — 'If you take one step, God takes two, or as many as He deems necessary, to bring you closer to what you want' — effectively separated me from the many in our world of opportunities. This mantra infused my mind, heart, and spirit, motivating me to continue being performance-driven and outcome-focused. One of my greatest assets was the ability to control my procrastination, distraction, and anxiety, putting my energy into planned outcomes.

My daughter was writing the initial draft of this book when my maxim, 'If you take one step, God takes two,' came up.

She would ask, "Dad, I understand what you are saying, but what does that mean?, in a peculiar manner. Living is just living".

So, as I stood in her room one day, I saw a sign that read, "Wake up, get up, dress up, show up, act up, and never give up." That sign was a deep dive into my soul. It spoke truth to power about me. Quitting isn't in my DNA.

I said, "Sweetheart, this is what I mean when I say, "If you takeone step, God will take two or more," while experiencing a strong inner serenity. Although I did not write those lines, they captured my thoughts and actions at the time. I told her that although I believe most of us know what to do, too few are willing to do what we know. My first step was recognizing the necessity of being diligent. In other words, having a performance and outcome-focused mentality, I will not allow self-interruptions (laziness, procrastination, distractions, and anxiety) to interfere with my focus and the planned course of action and milestones (POAM) result.

God blessed me with the awareness that I must get up, pursue my passion, and discover my mission when I am diligent in my life's work. This is how I express my gratitude to God for granting me this opportunity. Everyone has a choice. When God wakes me up, I have two options: I can roll over and continue sleeping, or I can get up, get dressed, appear presentable, and do whatever else is necessary to be present in whatever I am doing. The important phrase is, 'There's nothing left to do but do it.' It is about being dependable, goal-oriented, and performance-driven. The message is never to surrender.

With each obstacle, I did not regret falling behind, regaining my footing, and advancing. I refer to it as readapting or, if necessary, reinventing myself.

Typically, self-pity can turn into a routine, and at that point, you begin to forget yourself. I would be nothing more than a collection of excuses in six months, one year, or two years. Or, I could have been executing my plan of action and milestone (POAM) and achieving planned outcomes for six months, a year, or two years during the entire time frame. All because I decided to proceed and took the initiative to do so.

I resisted allowing a pity party mentality or portrayal of a character who departs when confronted with my traumatic car accident experience. It took some time, but I eventually gathered myself, approached it in my way, and did not allow it to become anything other than what it was: a period of recuperation.

It took me several months, not years, to recover from a head-on collision, but I regained the functionality of my mind, body, and soul due to my perseverance and strength of will. Physicians had suggested that regular use of the same leg was unlikely to recover. I had my usual private conversation with God, made the best effort possible to take the one step or portion thereof, and then the flow of blessings began. My greatest efforts consisted of always having faith in God and never giving up. My Lord took additional steps for me after I took my initial step. I stopped counting. I simply continued to run, leap, and call his name. My worst-case scenario was that the physicians saw only what they could see with their own eyes and that their dire predictions were accurate. The ideal scenario was that I was successful in attaining my objectives.

Readjusting to normalcy

I disagree with the assertion that the time spent rejuvenating was wasted time. My beliefs are uncomplicated. Any time spent producing physical, emotional, intellectual, or professional progress contributes to success. I declare as Earnest Henley does in his poem 'Invictus: I am the master of my fate; I am the captain of my soul.' During my recovery period, I learned valuable lessons, such as the significance of discipline in taking the first step toward doing something unpleasant or painful to accomplish my goal. This perspective assisted me in shaping my destiny and advancing toward a fortunate existence.

The tragedy, however, derailed those plans, initially. I regained full use of my legs by adhering to my personal trainer's and rehabilitation specialist's recommendations. For me, going through a rehabilitation procedure in which I had few options if I wanted to recover was both mentally and physically challenging. I respect the intellect's capacity to control the body because it enabled me to recover faster and better.

Occasionally, what you perceive to be the worst possible event can turn out to be a blessing in disguise. In addition to the lessons I learned from my rehabilitation experience, I was fortunate to receive an insurance settlement as a consequence of the accident. My college fund required assistance due to my community's mediocre socioeconomic status at the time, for lack of a better term.

I've always believed that if I attended college, I would complete my studies and be able to support myself and my family. I have always believed that perseverance, a quality education, and smart labor, wrapped in God's favor, are the keys to my upward mobility. I was resolute in taking the steps necessary to make it happen. God enabled me to earn two postgraduate degrees in addition to my undergraduate degree. The accident settlement enabled me to pursue my goal of obtaining a higher education, albeit with some obstacles.

I accepted the insurance payout as the unexpected gift that it was. I chose to continue to Chicago and start college rather than waste money and time on mourning parties in the beautiful city of Belgrade. This decision was simplified by the support of my brother Reander (Duke) and two of my cousins, Adam and Collon. We all lived and worked in the environment as brothers.

In my first year of college, I focused on mathematics in preparation for a career in engineering. I studied for approximately one and a half years or three semesters, earning 27 credits and a 3.50 GPA. Another setback, however, caught me by surprise and led me down a path that shaped me into the person I am today. Due to administrative and credentialing issues, the Chicago institution I attended lost its accreditation, and the credits I earned during my year and a half there were non-transferable.

The loss of transferability of earned college credits due to an issue with the designated college office can be a painful setback. I was determined, however, not to allow this detour to impede my plans. I felt comfortable turning to my private conversation with my Lord, and I was immediately referred to the inner strength and insights gained during my upbringing and acknowledging my ancestor's challenges, I suddenly recognized that, even though I was angry, and surely, I was, quitting simply wasn't in my DNA. My strengths were aligned with self-discipline, aspiration, inspiration and motivation, focused on planned outcomes. I accepted the roadblocks and decided to live by choice, refusing to allow hatred or fury to cloud my judgment or derail my objectives.

Instead of using an alibi, I decided to change careers and began searching for work in the hospitality industry while considering my next steps. I was unaware that I would interact directly with this nation's most hostile underbelly daily, weekly, and monthly for several years.

I met Mr. Peter Schruender not long after accepting a position at the Essex Inn in Chicago; he would go on to serve not only as my mentor but also as my ally, coworker, and lifetime friend. Mr. Schruender was a senior hotel administrator who was German born and worked at the Essex Inn. He had a lot of information and, as a white foreigner, was less susceptible to racial prejudice against Black Americans. Mr. Schruender did not permit his skin color to contaminate his mind with hatred, ignorance, and stupidity as it had done to a sizeable percentage of the white population of the U.S. in thepast, during those years (the 1960s, 1970s, and 1980s), and continuing into the twenty-first century, Mr. Schruender noticed something about me that I was already aware of but had never really thought about. "Derk, you worked well with people, learned quickly, have good judgment, and were loyal with integrity," he said at the time. He had the gall to advance me into the hotel management field, breaking through that ethnic wall of defense.

Peter Schruender, provided me the key, opened the door and guided me into the white world of Hotel Management. When he hired me, an African American who was a target for hotel management in an all-white hotel operation, he had no idea that he was about to embark on creating history with me.

The statements that follow are those of Mr. Peter Schreuder.

"Here is My American Story".

"Hello, my name is Peter Schruender, and I was born in 1936 in Germany. I had just turned nine when the Second World War ended in 1945. I recall when American troops passed through my hometown on tanks and massive vehicles. The troops waved back and grinned as we did. I recall that we also saw black men for the first time during this period.

I immigrated to the U.S. at the age of 21 after thirteen years. I was raised in a totalitarian country, Germany. Before the war, we only saw and heard what Adolf Hitler, the Fuehrer, intended us to see and hear. When most of the news came from the United States, that soon changed.

Most of us began to adore and respect the United States of America and all it stood for. A democratic nation with universal liberties, or so we thought. When I decided to immigrate to the United States, I was probably 12 or 13 years old—a democratic nation with equal chances. I had great success. Since her early years, my mother has known a doctor who resided and worked in North Dakota. Dr. Vonnegut was his title. He would occasionally travel to Germany to see friends and relatives. When he came to Muenster, my birthplace, my mother met him and introduced us. I engaged him in a protracted conversation in English, which I had acquired while residing and working on a farm in England between 1956 and 1957.

I took advantage of the chance and asked him if he could assist me in moving to the United States. One of the two North Dakota senators he called was someone he knew. I was the happiest man alive when I got a letter from the American Embassy in Frankfurt with emigration application papers and a request to visit them.

Are you a Homosexual? is one of the intriguing questions they still make me recall to this day. Do you wish to travel to America to topple the authorities? So much for that; I got the go-ahead to leave the country in just two weeks. I couldn't be happier. I flew from Duesseldorf, Germany, to Chicago on a Lufthansa aircraft (this was before jets) two weeks later, on April 19, 1958. The journey, which stopped in Newfoundland and Montreal, took 22 hours.

I was gathered up at Midway Airport by Dr. Vonnegut, who had assisted me with my emigration, his wife, and a couple from Chicago before they drove me into the city. I noticed tens of thousands of black men walking toward Chicago as we exited the airport. Who are these guys? I inquired. They responded that they were just inconsequential nitwits leaving the office. Nigger startled the hell out of me. It sounded extremely offensive, even though I had never heard it before. We had supper when we got to downtown Chicago, and then they dropped me off at the YMCA, where I spent the first few weeks of my stay in the city.

I got a position at the Bismarck Hotel as a busboy. I had a job that ran from 7 am to 3 pm. After working as a busboy, I asked the front desk manager if I could learn to be a desk clerk. Unbelievably, they elevated me to Desk Clerk within a few weeks, and I left my position as a Bus Boy.

I cherished Chicago. It was my 'hometown' in America. The populace of 'Muenster,' my hometown in Germany, was somewhere around 80,000. With almost four million residents, Chicago was, therefore, enormous. All the people, vehicles, and subways appeared to be operating. I found it to be extremely exciting. The majority of people were gracious and cordial toward me. I put a lot of effort into it, and eventually, I was able to get rid of my British dialect and sound more 'American.'

The reality that Chicago had two different racial populations—white and black—was a depressing aspect of America for me. They had varied lifestyles, lived in various parts of the city, and earned different amounts of money. The lodgings told the same tale. Nearly all of the staff members who interacted with guests in front of the hotel were white, while the majority of the staff members who interacted with guests in the rear of the building were black.

My work was successful. I left the Bismarck Hotel after a few years to work at the 350-room Essex Inn on South Michigan Avenue. As an assistant manager, I was employed. I was promoted to General Manager after holding the job for a while.

My acquaintance with Derk Mattocks began in 1968. He applied for the Essex Inn's Night Manager and Night Auditor positions. I was concerned because, in the 1960s, hiring African Americans to work in a hotel's front office was extremely uncommon, even in a big convention city like Chicago. However, I thought Mr. Mattocks would be able to manage the position well because he seemed very self-assured with good interpersonal skills. Over time, Mr. Mattocks developed into a highly skilled and productive manager who earned the respect of his staff and company management.

On the evening of Wednesday, April 3, 1968, however, at around 11:30 pm, I was going around the hotel. In the foyer, I ran into our Banquet Manager. We had a lengthy conversation outside the front office close to the lift. Our front office manager, Derk Mattocks, was manning the front desk. Like he always did, he presented a competent image.

The elevator door started to open at this moment. A senior guy exited the elevator carrying a younger man.

The older guy approached the desk and placed the key there, and asked Derk, after turning to face him, "What are you doing here? This is a profession for white men. Don't touch my key, Nigger!"

Together with his companion, he stood further away from the elevator and occasionally glared with hatred and disdain at Mr. Mattocks, calling him Nigger or Hey Nigger. I just stood there and observed this show. There was absolutely nothing I could have done to stop it. It would have been pointless to call the police because they would have treated African Americans about as poorly as the elderly man who had insulted Derk. I observed Derk during this roughly 20-minute stretch of continuous insults; he maintained a professional demeanor. He didn't speak or display any expression, which was truly amazing."

About 50 years later, being in front of that verbal assault, I remember the experience and pain very well. What Mr. Schreuder saw on my face was not, by any means, reflective of the words that were going through my mind and the pain and anger in my heart. What kept me anchored was Mr. Schruender's comments, "Derk, you work well with people, learn fast, and you have good judgment." I felt that was as good of a time as any to prove my worth by confirming his perception of me.

Ironically, a few hours after what Mr. Schruender witnessed that evening, a third, even younger (17 or 18) gentleman—and possibly a third-generation man traveling with those same two old men— became my hero.

This younger man came to the front desk thirty to forty five minutes later or so after the incident, as Mr. Schruender had described. He wanted to check out the Ascot Hotel, our sister property, which was situated several blocks south of the Essex Inn on the same street, Michigan Avenue. The younger man, who was by himself, asked for advice on how to get to the Ascot Hotel and whether to stroll or take a taxi.

"If you're alone, I advise calling a cab. However, since the weather is pleasant, you could stroll if you have company," I said.

He gave the impression that there would be a group before boarding the elevator to his room. I didn't know he was a member of the annoying pair who had demonstrated the dark undertones of that Jim Crow mentality until they passed through the lobby on their way to the Ascot hotel.

The younger man waved and said, "Thank you," but the other two continued walking as if nothing had occurred. Naturally, I nodded in response to his wave and thank-you from the younger guy.

An hour or so later, I walked home. My apartment was just two blocks south of the Essex Inn but a couple of blocks north of the Ascots Hotel. In other words, my apartment, also on Michigan Avenue, was between both hotels. However, I had gone to my apartment to pick up something and was walking back to the hotel. As I was leaving my apartment building, I was confronted by three black men. One of whom I recognized, as he was once friends with a young lady who had shifted her interest toward me. With fists raised, they began spreading out in an attempt to surround me. I was unaware that the three white men who had gone to the Ascot Hotel earlier were returning and were just behind me.

The younger gentlemen, about my height, walked directly up behind me and spoke with a confident voice, as if no one else was there, saying to me, "Hi, there you are. I was hoping that you had not left yet. I need to speak with you. Do you have a minute?"

He put his hand on my left shoulder, and we walked on to the Essex Inn, talking as if nothing had happened. The two men with him just walked along with us. When we entered the hotel, the younger gentleman gently hit my shoulder with his fist and said, "Have a good evening," and they all got on the elevator. He never did stop or come back to talk, at least while I was there. I never saw either of them again.

The real blessing was the young lad did not show any traits of having been contaminated with hate his associates had displayed earlier. I commend him for his maturity. The young lad left me with the confidence that, as Sam Cook would say, "A change is gonna come," the song playing on my radio when I was at my apartment. I truly hope, whatever their relationship, the two older men learned something too. My only regret is I will never know the outcome of the confrontation, as it never materialized.

When Mr. Schruender offered to put me in a position with greater responsibilities in the hotel, I felt obliged to let him know about my situation with my education. Mr. Schruender could see how distraught I was and made it comfortably clear to me that it was not a major issue.

Mr. Schruender took a huge step to motivate me by showing his belief and trust in me by putting me on a sequential and progressive training and professional development track. Starting as a night auditor, front desk clerk, and front desk manager, and following with some on-the-job training (OJT) in hotel, food, and beverage operations. Mr. Schruender felt that I was qualified for the positions and said I deserved the opportunities.

Though painful, my greatest challenge was not letting others' racial biases, hatefulness, and stupidity drive me to a hateful and likewise stupid mindset.

This was near the end of the 60s, closing out a decade in which we saw the assassination of President John F. Kennedy in 1963, the passing of the Civil Rights Act of 1964, the passing of the Voting Rights Act of 1965, and the assassination of Martin Luther King, Jr. in 1968, among many other noteworthy events. These events caused major social disruptions. It was a time of political and racial turmoil.

The hotel where I worked was amid the Democratic National Convention of 1968, one of the most politically charged events in history. One can imagine that any rational person might think it was less than ideal for me, a black man, to be working at the front desk of a major hotel at such a critical time, much less in charge of the front office.

The hotel owners expressed their concerns to Mr. Schruender that they were uncomfortable having a black person at the front desk. I would surmise that the owners had a greater interest in the hotel losing business than worrying about my safety. To his everlasting credit, Mr. Schruender proved to be a strong ally and stuck to his commitment, believing that I was the right person to handle the hotel front office responsibilities.

While the hotel owners disagreed, Mr. Schruender, without having any inkling that he was making history, had made his decision and kept me at the front office. I did not know Mr. Schruender that well at that time. I was impressed with his commitment to staying the course. It was apparent to him that my personality, work ethic, positive attitude, and skills were worthy of the position. Mr. Schreuder's words and actions aligned with him looking at me as nothing more than a man he felt could and would do the job. His words and actions were very much aligned with my teachings and upbringing.

Significantly, I began to witness the butt end of racial hate, ignorance, and stupidity, showing a high level of what I believed to be a mental deficiency, couched in mental illness. Fortunately, I learned early that accepting stagnation and/or degradation was not an option, even when outnumbered.

My regular private conversation with my Lord took me back to Mr. Schruender. In other words, if the boss, with the keys to the door, felt that I could do it, who am I to doubt his belief in me? So, I reverted to the mindset of, "Ain't nothing to it, but to do it." But making history was the furthest thing from my mind.

Telling My Story

A hotel management opportunity was a major turning point in my life. Few African Americans were working in the hotel industry above the level of housekeeper or bell captain, and certainly not in this type of high-profile management role. Rest assured, the opportunity was a great one, but the storm I faced during the 16-year journey was sometimes brutal.

The sustained tidal wave of racial hatred, based solely on and driven by ignorance and stupidity, inflicts mental, emotional, and physical pain, as well as financial pain on the innocen. And that racial hatred, ignorance, and stupidity proved just as damaging for businesses too.

So, I absorbed and placed those ongoing painful experiences in my briefcase. And, rather than fight the storm, I decided to dance in the rain. While I had many painful experiences, I gained insight from and considered each one as an inflow of wisdom. It helped open my mind and broadened my heart while making my eyes more useful for deeper insight into others' souls. I wrapped myself in my vision, focused on my success, visualized the image, did it often, and did the necessary work along the way. Many white patrons appeared disgusted when they asked to speak with the front office manager and were directed to me. Many simply refused to believe that I was the front office manager. I took it all in stride, recognizing that my ability to be calm, cool, and collected was among my greatest strengths. I knew my competence, patience, and professional duties could never be challenged. Many patrons, often reluctantly, followed through with whatever they may have needed my assistance with.

Those were some devastating experiences, and while the emotional pain from those experiences was intolerable, I managed. The insight I gained through dealing with such hateful people encouraged and made me more confident, competent, and courageous enough to put my pain in my briefcase and leave behind the disparaging experiences I was constantly subjected to. While I learned a lot about hateful people during those times, I failed to see any benefit in digging up the negative experiences that could only hinder my upward mobility. As there wasn't any reference that a black hotel manager on the white side of town had gone on before me, I was going where no black man or black woman had gone before. Every step on my hotel manager's journey was a first. I was just committed to following my mother's wisdom, reflecting on her guidance when she would say, "Stay calm and in command of yourself, and you will find out just how easy it is to get along, get things done, and grow." To that end, I sought even more deeply to understand myself, helping me avoid and manage negative and limiting beliefs and enabling me to focus more on my strengths. I recognized early in life how negative and limiting beliefs can impact one's mindset and quality of life. Recognizing and acknowledging that I was in charge and control of my mindset and quality of life was powerful. That recognition served as my superpower.

Several months later, Mr. Schruender was recruited by Ramada Inns Inc. as the Midwest Regional Director, responsible for 13 hotels. Mr. Schruender recruited me and sent me to the Ramada Inn's Hotel Training Academy, in Arizona, for new hotel managers.

When I attended the Ramada Inns Inc Hotel Training Academy in the early 70s, I immediately observed that I was the only African American of 27 in attendance. When reviewing the wall displaying classes of graduates who had gone on before me, I was unable to find one picture of an African American among all several hundred displayed on that wall.

Following graduation, I was assigned as Assistant General Manager to the 350-room Ramada Inn Hotel in St. Louis, Missouri, at Lambert Airport.

I recall those days fondly with much admiration for my friend and mentor, Peter Schruender, as that was, in my estimation, minus a few racial biases' hiccups, the best job I ever had.

As Assistant General Manager, I managed day-to-day hotel, food, and beverage operations, while the General Manager handled the politics and other external issues.

I managed contracts with several airlines, housing airline staff and offering packages to fill rooms with tourists and business visitors. There were many executive meetings where I organized and facilitated the agenda, reserving the right to have the last word, but often rarely needed to.

A year or so after this Assistant General Manager assignment, I was promoted to General Manager at the Ramada Inn in Clayton, Missouri. This was an even more prestigious position. There were many high-end guests because the hotel was in the financial district of Missouri.

When I was promoted to General Manager for the Ramada Inn, Clayton, Missouri, I was the only African American General Manager within the Ramada Inn chain, which consisted of some 600 hotels. Ramada, during that period, ranked as the second-largest hotel chain in the U.S. behind industry leader Holiday Inns, Inc., where I also searched but could not find an African-American hotel General Manager. Even when attending Ramada Inns annual conventions and executive meetings, I, as an African American, was the lone wolf. Likewise, when attending the American Hotel & Motel Association conferences in the early 70s, I again found myself, as an African American, the lone wolf.

My tenure, as General Manager, at the Ramada Inn, Clayton, Missouri, lasted for nearly three years. After the Ramada Inn, Clayton assignment, I was recruited by Mr. Jerry Sikes of the United Hotel Management Company (UHMC) of Chicago to be General Manager of Century Twenty-one Hotel, an independent hotel located at 3rd and John Street, Champaign, Illinois, on the campus of the University of Illinois, Champaign Urbana. I knew Mr. Sikes as a senior hotel executive from my days working at the Essex Inn in Chicago. He, too, was an excellent example of a mentor, leader, and ally.

The Century 21 hotel, a high-end 21-story high-rise, was located on the University of Illinois, Champaign Urbana campus. The Century 21 hotel housed the popular restaurant and lounge known as the Brass Rail Steaks N Stuff on the 21st floor; 270 up-scaled hotel rooms, 12 of which were executive suites, a coffee shop, and banquet facilities that accommodated 221 seated for a formal dinner. Included in that hospitality group was a discotheque named The Giraffe, which accommodated 300.

Following just under two years at Century Twenty-one, I switched hotel brands when I was recruited by Mr. Benny Williams, an African American and V.P. for Human Resources, and Mr. Brian Goodwin, a Caucasian, and I believe Sr. Vice President for Operations for the Holiday Inns Inc., headquarters, Memphis, Tennessee.

With some jubilation, I accepted the offer and forged ahead with an eight-year career with Holiday Inns Inc.

My first assignment with Holiday Inns Inc. was that of General Manager for the Holiday Inn high-rise in Jacksonville, Florida, in 1975, where I combated and maneuvered many challenges associated with reduced demand and changing business environments associated with the infamous 1975 gasoline shortage; Moreover, some mindless individuals who for some ungodly reason felt that I would be interested in their uttering perceived superiority and white privilege compounded my efforts somewhat.

Following my tenure at the Holiday Inn, Jacksonville, Florida, I was transferred to the Holiday Inn East, Columbus, Ohio. Several weeks after arriving at the Holiday Inn East assignment, I recognized a trend of low employee activity interfering with customer service. Initially, I attributed the low productivity to a lack of response to me, a new manager, disrupting habits of favored treatment. However, I soon realized there were three staff members, supervisory in nature, trying to influence other line employees, whose attitudes strongly suggested that they were privileged characters who thought they deserved special rights and advantages from me.

When querying several long-time employees on-site, I quickly concluded that these privileged characters never had such attitudes with any of my white predecessors. And that there had been conversations about my race. I called all three key staff members to my office at the same time and had two of them wait in my outer office until I finished with the first staff member. Excusing the first one, I called in the second staff member, but not before making sure the first had left for an airport assignment. Once I finished with staff member number two, I sent her on a downtown assignment while I spoke with staff member number three. After a short session with the third staff member, I placed on each staff member's desk a written plan of action and milestone (POAM) and an annotation that made it clear, in no uncertain terms, that if any one of them or all of them decided to stay on, I was open to discussion and willing to listen, but that I reserved the right to have the final say, until further notice. I informed each staff member that I would treat them as I treated all employees, with dignity and respect, and would not accept anything less.

A week or so following the meeting, I started facing challenges couched in politeness and smiles, which I would categorize as stealth racism. There was a lot of politics and some internal disregard for work ethic and basic integrity, but they finally calmed down, shaped up, and the standard of service spiked.

The increase in service levels coincided with an increased level of flirtation directed toward me by my secretary. I acknowledged that she had made mild advances before but thought she was joking. For some reason, she felt obliged to up the ante. Her attraction to me or action toward me became so overt that I felt damned if I submitted and damned if I refused to submit. Initially, she would flirt discreetly. When that didn't work, she became more open and boldly expressed her suggestive interest. I indicated that I was married, which she already knew, and that I was not by any means interested. Still, she continued her pursuit. However, when I suggested to her that I was not into white women, things shifted rapidly and not in a good way.

Instead of just leaving me be and stopping her advances, she decided to file a report with my boss, Mr. Jim Thompson, Regional Director, claiming that I was misappropriating funds. She had failed to realize that I didn't utilize my access to the safe and funds by choice. My boss, Mr. Thompson, had foreseen this as a possibility and advised me to set up a system for facilitating petty cash funds.

The only people with access to the safe were my assistant manager and my secretary, albeit with my permission, as they were my checks and balances. One did not have permission to enter the safe without the other one being present. When my boss came to investigate, I approved her suspension and subsequent termination since he knew that, by design, the system I set up didn't give me access to the petty cash funds. That was another life lesson for me. If there is someone you think might lead you down the wrong path, you must keep your vision clear, displaying complete honesty and openness. A dim vision can cause you to stumble, resulting in short-term satisfaction and long-term suffering. People, in general, and men in particular, have gone down that long path of short-term satisfaction and long-term suffering. As a strong believer in self-evaluation and self-regulation, my discipline prevailed.

While I certainly had the authority to make sure that no one else except me had access to the hotel funds, I didn't need access to make me feel important. However, I chose the complete honesty and openness vision route. In doing so, I kept my vision truly clear. And, in avoiding the person who wanted me to cheat, I earned the respect of my staff and bosses. I feel a person's true character is revealed when he stays the course regardless of whether someone is looking or not.

It didn't matter to me that she was Caucasian from Waco, Texas. At that time, it was hard for a Black person to win a case of "he said / she said" against a Caucasian person, but I, with pride and commitment, stuck to my guns. My integrity was more valuable to me than any job. Even so, that was a trying time for me. If a single person had believed her over me, I would have likely been fired and possibly sent to jail with my promising career ending. Fortunately, in this instance, truth prevailed.

Following that 24-month bump in the road, I was granted a transfer to Holiday Inn Georgetown in Washington, D.C.

My predecessor, who managed the Holiday Inn East, had lived in the house that was the hotel manager's quarters which was separate from the hotel. When I arrived and took over the Holiday Inn East, I asked that the house that I was to live in be cleaned. The Regional office informed me that they would have someone come in and do the carpets and the windows. I asked about having them clean the walls too.

I was told, "No one in the house smoked."

Puzzled by the response, I secretly hoped they would clean the walls and everything.

The contract workers, who cleaned my housing quarters following my predecessor moving out, did the bare minimum, which resulted in me having to pay, from my pockets, another crew who did a thorough cleaning.

However, when I finished my two-year assignment at Holiday Inn East, Columbus, Ohio, I was transferred to Holiday Inn Georgetown, Washington, D.C. Upon my departure from Holiday Inn East, Columbus, Ohio housing quarters, the Regional Office hired contractors to go to my former housing quarters and do just short of a full renovation for the new General Manager, who just happened to be a Caucasian female. Guess what? I didn't smoke, either. For me, it merely confirmed what I always experienced, blacks, regardless of who you are, matter far less, if at all, than whites in the hotel industry. I just thought that Holiday Inns, Inc., the largest in the industry, would have learned something during its growing pains, but racial sensitivity was not one of them. I put that pain in my briefcase, put a smile on my face, and refused to allow negative thoughts and disparaging experiences to derail my focus.

I acknowledge that I believe there will be those with built-in guilt and ongoing insecurities who think that the African-American community is somehow inferior to the Caucasian community. Likewise, I believe there will always be people, though few and far between, who will work hard to support fair play and help make life better for the least of us. Peter Schruender, Jerry Sikes, Bill Eccles, Jim Thompson, and even Brian Goodwin were great mentors, allies, and leaders to me while working in the hotel industry. A faction of people in the community would put up mental barriers because of some past incident or experiences.

However, in such times, I've always learned to show my strength, making sure I choose not to allow my emotions to be dictated by someone else's stigma or stupidity. As long as I know that I am fair with others, I do not apologize for having a point of view. I maintain my values, for no one can be truer to me than I can be to myself.

My upward mobile career (1968 – 1984) in the hotel industry was speedy, operating hotels in Chicago, Ill., Saint Louis, Mo., Clayton, Mo., Champaign, Ill., Jacksonville, Fla., Columbus Oh, Washington, DC and Gary, Ind. Therefore, when some guests asked to speak with a supervisor or manager, they often met with me. Often, when they realized they would be dealing with an African American, some were challenged with wrapping their minds around meeting a black man. They would then ask to speak with the General Manager. During the late 60s and early 70s, not wanting to or refusing to meet with me was a regular occurrence, a couple of times a week. I must admit that for more reasons than I will confess, I enjoyed the expression on their faces when they learned that I was General Manager. And I put a lot of emphasis on the word "general" while uttering 'General Manager.

The fact that I was the first African-American General Manager for a major white-owned brand hotel became quite popular after a while, and I got offers from several companies. The one offer that stood out most was an offer from Murphy's Hotel Corporation, a black entrepreneur in Washington, D.C. Ed Murphy, with the help of D.C. and the federal government, had built a prominent boutique-like upscale hotel called the Harambee House Hotel, adjacent to the campus of Howard University.

Mr. Murphy, the President of Murphy's Hotel Corporation, sought to recruit me to be General Manager for the Harambee House Hotel. So, he sent a team to Holiday Inn, Georgetown, Washington, D.C., where I was the hotel General Manager, tasked with convincing me to come on board at the Harambee House Hotel. I thought it was a great idea to be an African American, operating a hotel owned by an African American adjacent to Howard University, a prominent historically black college and university (HBCU) in the D.C. area. That was an opportunity and philosophy that seemed promising to me. I accepted, and it resulted in a very productive operation.

This was a fantastic opportunity for me because not only was I contributing to successful business operations but also contributing to the community culture.

I soon realized on this assignment how much I had learned during my time under the tutelage of my mentors and allies, Peter Schruender, Jerry Sykes, Jim Thompson, and Bill Eccles, when I joined the Harambee House operation. I learned that I had been mentored and trained by the best of the best in hospitality management.

The Harambee House, an upscale hotel, minority-owned, had far fewer resources than those owned by major brand hotels like the

Holiday Inn, Ramada Inn, and Sheraton Hotels. However, we turned that hotel into a successful operation with the right leadership and using time, money, and effort efficiently and effectively.

The single most important thing I learned early in my life was great listening skills. I believe that one of the greatest assets you can have in the service industry, as in any industry, is knowing how to be present to the person who is asking or telling you something.

My listening skills enabled me to respond with clarity of understanding. I strongly feel my ability to listen, even though I may disagree, has served as one of the skills that helped make me successful. Some experiences, racial in nature, left me hurt, even angry, but I refused to be bitter or to worry. I figured it was a total waste of my time. It wouldn't change anything. So, I refuse to allow their stupidity to steal my joy. I just chose to prove that I was stronger, smarter, and better.

Other than that, listening was also a skill that helped me both personally and professionally. I learned to be attentive and flexible. It is also a beneficial skill when it comes to learning and developing a plan of action and milestones (POAM) for the hotel. It feels good when you can be in an environment where the people around you are so comfortable that your presence just blends in. I had many experiences where I felt as if I were a fly on the wall. Even though I was the only African American there, I often would hear things or observe situations that, I strongly suspect, were not meant for my eyes and ears – some good and some not so good. I quickly learned to be an ethical chameleon.

I found that my silence was one of my greatest tools. During sessions in which I was present, it was as if they had forgotten I was there. However, having an open mind can always be a great advantage, and I believe even more so when you are in an executive or managerial position.

In essence, I learned a lot from those insightful experiences. The ability to listen and know the value of doing so while keeping an open mind is priceless. During my career, my discipline, listening, observing, and assessment skills had divided into two types of situations: Situation one was those who, when one-on-one, just liked and wanted to talk. More often than not, my listening style created an environment leading them to tell me things about others, then their friends, and, in due time, themselves. Situation two was when participating in group sessions, in a conference environment, or with someone else minding our business but near others having their conversation. Many would be surprised to know what you can hear when others who don't value your presence forget you are there.

And once they recollect, they will say, "But you are different!"

While I have never participated in drugs, alcohol, or any mind-altering substances, I would submit that if anyone reviewed a period in which they were under a mind-altering substance, regardless of how mild it was, they would give some serious thought to such practice. I assure you my observation confirmed there's a chance you will do things you wouldn't normally do while sober. In any case, the majority of insights I gained proved valuable to friendship, personal or professional relationships, and other entities as appropriate. It was an experience I would imagine a fly on the wall goes through.

Mr. Schruender would say, "Derk, your consciously quiet mannerism creates such a welcoming environment that gives you access to a lot of people, places, and things."

I would share my perspective on the art of listening with him, indicating that it isn't that difficult but requires a purposeful effort.

However, while I was learning the art of listening, I also realized that I had to be prepared to hear things that were not always meant for my ears. Some things were insightful and served my purpose. Other times, it was about me, fell into the good, the bad, or the ugly category, and made me slightly enraged sometimes. Still, other times, what I heard was bigger than me, requiring it be elevated to proper entities (corporate management or appropriate level of law enforcement), as appropriate. Still, I knew that being calm, cool, and collected was valuable to maintaining decorum, no matter the setting.

The oppression of the African American community was overtly heinous, as the treads of racism shrouded and hunted my DNA from the slave trade to slavery, reconstruction, Jim Crow, the Civil Rights movement, the 1964 Civil Rights Act, and moving with warped speed into the 21st century.

As the first African-American General Manager of an international brand white-owned hotel, I recognized that there could be many changes. Still, many changes were supposed to come. While the why and where were clear, the who, how, and when were the questions and works in progress. All I knew at the time was that I had a hold of something that I intended to hold on to, come hell or high water.

Being the first Black hotel manager, this was my way of seeing and hearing the reality of what I termed stealth racism. I acknowledged the broad smiles and politeness but refused to accept the distortion of facts, withholding of needed-to-know information, and the passing on inaccurate or false information to me or about me or relevant to areas under my leadership, regardless of their smiles and politeness.

Considering myself to be both quantitative-minded and qualitative-expressive, I would shift into an analytical and assessment mode, eliminating the jargon and pleasures and sticking with and investigating common facts. When the facts were re-established, the distortion of false or unshared information always came back to my skin color. The color of my skin was such a big deal at the time that it was used as a silent and subtle threat bent on isolating me.

However, my inner strength enabled me to hold on by tooth and nail, and sometimes by just a string, but I held on. I was in an environment that neither my associates nor I were used to. So, it was a teaching moment, and I did teach. I knew there had to be a change, so I initiated an approach to bridge the gap.

Running a hotel is complex. Building teams within a team, planning, organizing, leading, delegating, and using resources efficiently and effectively are all musts. Framing the organization's vision and supporting it with its mission and purpose, setting goals, laying out objectives, sharing values, and developing metrics focusing on hotel guest satisfaction is the process that yields success.

For my part, all this was done through a performance-driven and customer-focused attitude which included professional and attentive staff, clean rooms, a clean building and clean grounds, great food, multi-flavored beverages, and entertainment, augmented with amenities, such as a pool, hot tubs, sauna facility, an exercise room, gaming area for the kids, complimentary breakfast, etc. Fortunately, or unfortunately, they did not have wireless Internet services, so I did not have to worry about wireless Internet services at any additional cost.

Successful outcomes were couched in the manager's ability to plan and execute well, ensuring expenses were proportionately less than incomes, thereby realizing sufficient profit was just some of my bosses' attention-getters. Yes, as I said, a lot went into running a hotel, which is a group of businesses within a business, all centered around the organization's vision, mission, goals, objectives, values, and metrics.

Staying abreast of which elements of the hotel meet its goal as it relates to forecasts when compared to budget, and what to do about it when it isn't, is paramount to the manager's success. However, just imagine, in my case, where I had been subjected to overt and covert discrimination on a daily, weekly, monthly, and annual basis, and through it all, I held my head high and performed equal to or greater than my white peers

I was alert and attentive, with greater-than-normal analytical skills. I was customer-driven and service-focused on efforts to achieve successful hotel operations outcomes. I wholeheartedly accepted that I intentionally left out somethings that would have been too problematic for me (racist stupidity), other than a minor nuisance if I had succumbed to the horrible, prejudiced mindset that permeated the hotel industry during my 16 years working in the industry.

Nevertheless, more than any other, one experience left me shocked and posed my greatest challenge to recover from such racist stupidity. While I initially refused to elaborate on many experiences, I credit my daughter with refusing to accept my leaving out such demeaning experiences as I had done with her on so many other prejudicial narrow-minded situations that I had been subjected to. So, my daughter hemmed and hawed until she made me realize, she is like me; quitting is not in her DNA. She made it clear, in no uncertain terms, she felt my pain as I began talking. She admitted insights she gained from interviewing me enabled her to recognize how torn I was. She saw the pain in my eyes. I had to regroup and speak up.

My daughter always saw me, while not perfect, as a strong, kind, humble man who happened to be black. For me, her need to know the cause of my pain won out.

I started with, "Sweetheart, life can throw you your greatest curve when you least expect it. And more so when you are least prepared for it."

I prepared myself to tell her about this particular experience. I went on by saying that while I consider myself mentally and physically strong, I was blessed with the experience I am about to share with you, an experience that tested my DNA and continues to do just that. I thank God for an experience that showed me how to put my pain and anger caused by a fight for equity and social justice, on my back, using Civil Rights principles as my guide, aspiration, inspiration and motivation as my drive, and focus on adversity, something that I can manage, as my target. The experience served to open my mind providing better insight, enabling me to find a better physical sight, and making me better prepared to deal with adversity in such turbulent times.

I went on to tell my daughter while General Manager at the Holiday Inn, Jacksonville, Florida, I was host to the 1975 Shriners conference, an organization I understood to be associated with Freemasons. Although this group was a well-recognized non-profit organization that helped hospitals, charities, and such, my experience with some of them was disappointing. I soon realized, based on some members' rude and disrespectful actions, there was a character flaw in some of the brothers and wondered how contaminated its membership could be, as proved to be the case when my African American staff and I had to work with several guests who were Shriners members.

I would never have thought people with such an organization who are "doing" such great work would have such a disregard for treating people of any race with dignity and respect.

The way some of the participants conducted themselves at the hotel conference was rather embarrassing. Some treated some of my staff and me, who are black, rudely for no apparent reason other than our skin color.

As I brought it to the attention of my contact person with the Shriners, who handled the booking, that person shook it off, saying, "That doesn't sound like any of our members," and walked away.

A member standing near and hearing my complaint pointed out another member standing at the front desk, indicating that the person was close to the Shriner's leadership. As I approached this member, noted as being close to leadership, I witnessed this individual berating one of my desk clerks, who was also African American. I proceeded to run interference and offer assistance, only to find that the African-American desk clerk had stepped forward to wait on this particular member. The person he preferred to have waited on him was a Caucasian female desk clerk who, at the time, was busy on the phone.

I introduced myself as a General Manager and asked, "May I help?"

My attempt to intervene fell on deaf ears. I asked a second time pointedly and got a response. Without direct eye contact, the Shriner member said, "And what can someone like you do for me?" And then walked away.

It was the emphasis on "someone like you" that spoke to his delusional mindset and pejorative demeanor that told us more about him than he would ever know about my staff, behind the counter, and me. Embarrassed by the Shriner member's stupidity, I apologized to my staff, pulled the file, checked the number, and called the Shriner's office, but I got no answer. I searched the premises until I found the original contact person I spoke with earlier and dealt with when finalizing the booking.

As he and I walked back to my office, we both witnessed the same guest asking others in his immediate group, without any checked voice, "Is a "black" hotel the best we could have done?"

The member walking with me walked over to this group as I stood by his side and asked, "Are there any problems or concerns, Mr. Mattocks, or I can help you with?"

You could hear a pin drop. The group of seven to ten members dispersed. The gentleman walking with me was the same person I had spoken with first.

The same person who said, "That doesn't sound like any of our members," apologized profusely.

I never mentioned to the contact person that another member standing within earshot of the member berating my desk clerk was the deputy of the local organization and was talking with a local politician, and yet, neither one, while aware, would make eye contact or say a word. Though not that close, these two people were in proximity to the group the contact person and I had a mild encounter with. And again, I said that he is unaware of any action(s) taken or comments made by leadership addressing the issue. I was thinking, how could senior participating members who represented such a "caring and giving organization" be so insensitive and uncaring when they were aware or should have been aware of such overt biases and chose to say nothing was disappointing, shocking, and hurtful. Hurtful only because their silence was couched in the delusional disorder of superiority. Their actions, or lack thereof, spoke volumes to the broad contamination of hate, ignorance, and stupidity within the group.

The more I observed and interacted with the "group" that weekend, the more painful the experience was. I coached my staff, including my Caucasian staff, not to allow the conference members' antics to impose racial trauma on them. As often as I had done before, I was able to put my direct pain and anger in my mental briefcase. But there was such a lingering piercing pain that wouldn't let go. For some reason, I could not rid myself of that pain. It soon struck me that the pain I felt was from the trauma I witnessed being inflicted on my innocent staff, and I didn't have a briefcase large or tight enough to house that pain. I could not protect them.

Because I was unable to rid my black staff of their pain, I had to stay in a relentless and ongoing private conversation with my God to harness my angry and violent thoughts while smiling all the way. I've carried that feeling with me for some time. I was even advised to talk with someone about the experience to help me close that chapter in my life. While it has been a tug of war, I have managed to put it in the back of my mind. I dealt with the challenge by going back within, seeking a deeper and better understanding of myself, reflecting on how I had taught myself to avoid and manage negative and limiting beliefs, and focusing more on my strengths.

During the process, I decided to give the racist stupidity the benefit of the doubt. I recall some readings I had done earlier in my life when studying the science of neuro-linguistic programming (NLP): "A brain will constantly rewire itself to suit the information that you feed it. So, if you constantly complained, felt anger, found excuses, etc.; your brain would make it easier for you to find issues to be upset about, regardless of what is happening around you. Likewise, if you constantly search for opportunities, abundance, love, and things to be grateful for, it will make it much easier for you to find a reflection of those things around you."

God knows it took practice, but over time the experience was very powerful in reshaping my reality. My reality positioned me to reflect on Hope as the one thing that is stronger than Fear. Life is tough. To be tougher than life itself, I needed to garner the power of Hope to push through difficult times and succeed, as quitting was not in my DNA. Reflecting on what my Ancestors would do, I resurrected the deep pain within me and identified an outlet, giving it a place to live external to my mind, body, and spirit.

I chose to continue my pursuit of higher learning, strengthening my capacity to lead, consult, advise, and lead, opening more minds, pointing out what's in it for them, and converting and winning over once hateful and intolerable souls.

My journey into the Masonic fraternity started with acceptance and being elected President of my class. Our team was unified, achieving proficiency at each educational stage—E.g., in the First Degree-Entered Apprentice, Second Degree-Fellowcraft, and Third Degree-Master Mason Degree. As a Master Mason and proud member of Charles H. Wesley Lodge No. 147 Prince Hall, F.&A.M., over the years, I cannot, for the sake of me, identify an inkling of any education or behavior reflecting my experience with the various Masonic men and their racist antics during my Jacksonville Florida Holiday Inns experience.

Only when my daughter started interviewing me for the book, smiling, she said, "Don't leave out the juicy stuff ."

I shared many experiences, yet I was unable to talk about my 1975 experience hosting the Shriner convention at the Holiday Inn Jacksonville, Fla.

As a Masonic member for several years, I consulted with a senior Masonic brother about my Shriner experience. He was straightforward and advised:

"Brother Mattocks, it was your experience; it's your decision. Put it in your book or leave it out. Whatever you choose to do, talk to someone about the experience."

If hosting the Shriner convention at the Holiday Inn Jacksonville, Florida, in 1975 had been my first hotel experience dealing with such hateful and delusional behavior of people representing such an organization as guests, I might have left the hotel industry.

However, the fact that I was a seasoned hotel manager, I wasn't about to let all of my hard work and knowledge go down the drain just because of a few hateful, ignorant, and disrespectful behaviors, creating a bump in my career path.

As I had already learned from reading Kurt Vonnegut, "Be soft. Do not let the world make you hard. Do not let pain make you hate. Do not let the bitterness steal your sweetness. Take pride that even though the rest of the world may disagree, you still believe it to be a beautiful place."

I learned how to put my pain in my briefcase, chose to be patient, and ensured they got the superb level of service my hotel provided.

As I was nearing the last months of my contract with the Murphy Hotel Corporation and the Harambee House Hotel, I was approached by Judge Douglas Grimes, President of Steel Plaza Inc., in Gary, Indiana. I soon learned that Judge Grimes was a real Judge; hence the Hon. Judge Grimes was a senior partner and President of Steel Plaza Inc., owner of the Sheraton Hotel franchise in Gary, Ind. Judge Douglas Grimes recruited me to join his organization as General Manager of their Sheraton Hotel in Gary, Indiana. I was receptive to that offer, and after finishing my tenure at the Harambe House Hotel, I switched, accepting his offer. This was the second major hotel owned by an African-American organization for whom I worked.

The Hotel Sheraton, Gary, and Ind worked in coordination with the local convention center. At the time, the convention center was finishing construction. I handled the hotel successfully, hosting conference events, parties, and hotel guests.

Two-and-a-half years was normally my duration for working at a hotel. However, two years into my G.M. assignment at the Hotel

Sheraton, an individual with the agency, U.S. Army Community and Family Support Center (USA CFSC) of the Department of Army, approached me to be considered for a hotel management position in Seoul, Korea. This was quite a surprise and a huge opportunity since they asked me to operate a hotel on a Military Installation in Seoul, Korea.

Also, I found this odd, as I didn't remember having ever filled out any kind of application for a job posting in Seoul, Korea.

Nor was I familiar with any type(s) of hotels they had in Seoul, Korea, or anywhere else. Soon, though, I found out that an Army Colonel named Col. Daughtry, someone I did not know, had referred me. I was called for an interview, went for it, and was offered the job. However, just before I departed for Seoul, USACFSC changed my destination to Frankfurt, West Germany. I was informed that leadership preferred assigning me to Frankfurt, West Germany, because of my broad experience in hotel, food & beverage, marketing, and financial operations.

They framed it as an assignment where I would coach, train, and advise executives, managers, and supervisors on Military Installations, throughout the European region. I was informed that I would be responsible for leading a team or being part of a team, going to Military Installations, and consulting with the business program managers of that particular installation. The programs included hotels, clubs, restaurants, bowling, and golf, among other businesses.

I accepted the job offer and served 25 years with the U.S. Army Community and Family Support Center (USACFSC), Department of Defense (DoD) Agency, retiring in 2006. I served 16 of those years as a senior instructor and an advisor at USACFSC, headquarters at the Morale Welfare and Recreation (MWR) Business Management & Programs Academy in Falls Church, VA. I traveled throughout the United States, coaching, advising, and training senior managers and supervisors charged with operating business and program activities on Military Installations.

My previous assignment with USACFSC led me to USACFSC's European Regional Office (ERO), Frankfurt, West Germany, as Team Chief, Technical Assistant, and Management Analysis (TAMA), where, for nine years, I was charged with leading teams and advising Military Installations staff on strategic and business planning, quantitative and qualitative analysis, contract management, marketing, and human capital management for business and program operations throughout Europe, the Pacific Rim, the Middle East, and Africa, supporting our uniformed personnel who served anywhere and everywhere, ensuring that they receive the same quality of service they are so willing to defend.

I always felt that even though I was paid well for this job, my greatest satisfaction came from the opportunity to serve and support the armed forces. This was my second opportunity to serve, and I was more than happy to take on the assignment.

My past work experience was of immense importance when I got employed by the Military. The adventures I led, the hardships I had to overcome, and the ideals I formed during these years were vital in my quest to live an uplifting, moral, and ethical life. I always credited my successes to my hometown of Belgrade, my family, and the village lifestyle upbringing. And, of course, I also credit my good friend and mentor, Peter Schruender. Mr. Schruender supported my confidence, my competence, and my courage, all pillars of my successes, and couched in my listening and learning skills.

Throughout my life, I've been in the presence of those seniors who respected and appreciated my wit while continuing to share their insights. But then there were others, and there were many, who felt threatened by me for some ungodly reason, and that I was undeserving of whatever "it" was that they felt so privileged to. This privileged bunch invested more time than I thought was necessary to protect whatever "it" was they thought I wanted that was theirs.

The fact is that life goes on with or without them or me. Situations aren't always as clear as they seem. The world isn't black and white; it isn't rainbows and sunshine nor gloom and doom. However, as you get older, you learn to appreciate what others have done for you and how far along they have supported you at the expense of their own experiences.

CHAPTER 3

First African-American Hotel General Manager

The employment situation for the African-American community was always a challenge. A Black man seeking employment in the hospitality industry wasn't any different, except that the challenge was tougher because it was hospitality management. There were little to no opportunities for blacks. The jobs available were not stable enough. I was fortunate to have had such a great opportunity, but it was a difficult time for me. My society was going through a transitional phase. I now realize that change does not always have to be progressive. Change can also be painful. While I had chosen not to be bitter, no Black man at that time could have been untouched by the plight of African Americans.

Vacancies available in the hospitality and hotel management field were certainly not to available for blacks. Still, excusing the white hotel owners and employers for their blatant biases was unacceptable. Racial biases seemed to drive the mainstream White population against seeing a Black person drinking at a water fountain, and even more so when they entered a major hotel. Needless to say, neither Peter nor I, at the time, recognized it as a historic and noteworthy opportunity for me to have been recruited for the hotel management track.

Peter Schruender, my German friend, a hotel executive, and mentor, had recruited and shown me the ropes of the hotel business enough so that I could achieve several managerial positions, including General Manager positions in fine hotels.

Despite facing relentless intolerance up, down, and around the hospitality arena, Mr. Schruender supported my confidence, competence, and courage to learn and grow.

Only because I was a Black hotel manager, I was often subjected to prejudiced demeanor and actions from some general managers of other hotels, employees within hotels I operated, and customers, who often tried not to recognize me as General Manager, even though my goal was to help make their stay as pleasant as possible. Seeing a Black man in charge of a hotel operation was mentally challenging for many of these people.

For instance, when reflecting on my hotel career, St. Louis, Missouri, was one of the best and ideal hotels that I got to work at. However, while there, I experienced several blatant racial incidents. There was one particular incident that I never cared to talk about.

I was the Assistant General Manager at the Lambert Airport Hotel. The marketing director of that hotel happened to work for Mr. Schruender. The hotel catered to the airline personnel from Delta, TWA, etc. I knew many of the airline executives and personnel.

One young lady, an airline client, asked if I would join her for her friend's wedding. Her friend was the bride-to-be of the marketing director, Robert Fitzgerald. I indicated that I would think about it, as Robert himself has yet to invite me directly. However, Robert got wind of me being invited to his wedding and told the young lady who had invited me that he was reluctant to have blacks at the wedding. I didn't know why that feedback didn't surprise me, but it didn't. I thought about mentioning it to Peter but then decided not to, realizing that it was Robert's wedding and his wishes should be respected.

Unfortunately, tragedy struck the couple's fate post-wedding. Robert and his bride, following the wedding, were in a car accident, and his bride was killed. When I heard about the accident, I offered my sincere condolences and never said anything about not being invited to the wedding to anyone. However, that one incident made it clear to me what Robert had thought of me while working with me regularly. Assuming he didn't have black people there, it was his choice to have whomever he wanted at his wedding. I respected his decision.

I was subjected to racial bias regularly by customers, and then there were fractions amongst other managers and colleagues whose display of racial bias matched some of the customers' overtures. There was a lot of discomfort in clients' demeanor whenever they realized I was black and the manager of the hotel. As mentioned several times earlier, I was often a bigotry target, and most of the hate mainly came from white male clients. Most people were not a problem, but the ones who were, left unpleasant memories. During interviews with my daughter, I told her that it was almost as if they came prepared with an attitude intending to hit me where it hurt the most. It was more like, let's go in and irritate Mr. Mattocks, the Black hotel manager. It happened regularly and kept happening up until the last four years when I operated hotels catering to predominantly African-American clientele. But, as I told my daughter, the transition wasn't necessarily a cakewalk, as there were some blacks, men in particular, who had co-opted the white man's mentality, that of acting like other Blacks were inferior to them. I just let them enjoy their fake inflated mental shortcomings.

So, like always, I looked inward at what I could do better to improve situations and grow. For the first 10-12 years of my hotel career, my clientele was about 90 percent Caucasian. However, in the last four years, the situation has changed for people of color. The ratio dropped to 40 percent Caucasians and 60 percent people of color because of the demographics of (The Harambee House of DC and Hotel Sheraton of Gary, Ind) the hotel's communities.

The situation now is very different than when I was a young man. Today you'll see young African American people in every walk of life and every profession, even the President of the United States. However, I submit that while there are a few, the hotel industry is still out of step and lagging far behind when it comes to Blacks in the middle and upper levels of hotel management.

Times have changed, but still, in this day and age, some people are uncomfortable meeting and socializing with Black people. Maybe it's still because of their delusional superiority complex, or perhaps it's because some people are still locked into sincere ignorance and an absurd stupidity trap, but none of it makes sense. There's a very simple ideology that all men and women can follow when it comes to dealing with others: live and let live. It doesn't matter if someone is from a different ethnic, racial, religious, or any other background. They deserve to be treated with respect, and that goes for those you might falsely feel are beneath your station. It doesn't matter, even if it's a hotel bellhop. That's their job; it's not who they are. It's what they do. They deserve respect and to be treated with dignity.

My experiences over the years strongly suggest that racism, thinking you are superior because of your skin color, and entitled to privileges over others, show a level of ignorance and stupidity, making the individual a prime mental case. And until it's proven otherwise, that's my story, and I'm sticking to it. This holds for any other race, creed, or color who, too, subscribes to that superiority complex, and rest assured, I have met a few.

The fact that some people think that any race or identity is superior to any other, I submit, is nothing less than mental illness. In today's world, more than ever, you will find people from all walks of life, all races, creeds, nationalities, and gender identities from all over the world interacting in endless ways. Our first instinct should not be to judge others based on the color of their skin or where they came from. There are countless examples of people minding their own business yet being harassed or, worse, for no other reason except that they were different in some way.

This is why so many Black Americans live their lives in fear. They have this gut-wrenching, heartbreaking task of having to explain to their children that some people will treat them differently. They have to always be on guard to coach their children on how to protect themselves. Imagine having that conversation with your child, telling them how to protect themselves for no other reason than they were born black. Imagine a child's innocent mind trying to grasp that. It's truly a sad state of affairs, yet they need to be made aware of these facts because they need to be prepared for the world as it is, not how it should be.

There's no denying the fact that progress has been made in some areas. Th e impact of racial biases may appear a bit diminished to some extent as more opportunities are available to Black people and other marginalized individuals. But, has the situation improved? In some ways, yes, but we still have a long way to go.

I don't and will never advocate disproportionately favorable treatment for minorities, but I will fight for nothing less than a level playing field.

Peter Schruender, at his own risk, provided me with a level playing field, and I excelled. I chose not to live in fear because the color of my skin is something that I had no control over, something I was born with and cannot change. And yes, unapologetically, I do not want to change.

De facto inferiority is not in my DNA. Anyone who accepts being treated as inferior, allowing anyone to assume superiority because of the way they look or sound, can also be a part of the problem. The simple fact that some people might be fooled and conned doesn't make them an idiot. The idiot syndrome stems from blatantly refusing to look at the truth and consciously believing the lies. It benefits all races and cultures to respect every other race and culture and accept nothing less. I would submit that anyone who gives another person tacit permission to treat them as inferior is part of the problem of racial discrimination. Indeed, they, too, have co-opted the practice in support of bigotry.

At the end of the day, we all must realize that society needs to change, and no one can accomplish this task alone. We might be able to change ourselves, but everyone needs to change. As a part of a community, you can help bring about societal change by standing up for what you know is morally, ethically, and legally right. And even legally can be questioned sometimes. Remember, the slave trade and slavery were legal. Likewise, Jim Crow laws were state and local statutes that legalized racial segregation.

Jim Crow laws were a collection of state and local laws statutes that legalized segregation. Remember, these Jim Crow laws existed, on the books, for about 100 years, from the Post-Civil War era until 1968— They were meant to marginalize African Americans by denying them the right to vote, hold jobs, get an education, or other opportunities. The Jim Crow practices still exist in parts of the United States of America. To put it in perspective, it was 1968 when I, a young Black man, started my venture as a hotel General Manager in a White-owned and operated establishment. Just imagine his audacity! And I never looked back.

Unethical practices and flawed morals will always be a part of our society, whether we want it or not. We must always look at them from a legal and moral standpoint. For example, if you see a police officer interrogating a black man, you may feel inclined to intervene, but you are no less than a tiger's fool if you decide to do so. You could be making the policemen's job more complicated than it already is. Moreover, that police officer may have a legitimate reason for his actions.

However, a wiser course of action would be to exercise your right and due diligence to observe and document the interaction to ensure that the person is being treated fairly. This is just one example. Earlier in this book, Peter Schruender, my boss, indicated witnessing a verbal assault on me by a white man who was a guest in a hotel where I worked. Mr. Schruender noted that even though the weird act of berating me by that guest and disrupting the decorum of the hotel, he (Mr. Schruender) was afraid to call the police, feeling that the police would make the matter worse, with me a black man being on the rough end of the stick, no pun intended. And for no other reason than me being a black man.

We need to be honest, ethical, and fair in our interactions with others, no matter who they are or what they look like.

As an African American, one of the first things I talked about in this book was my DNA structure. All black people living in this world have a rich historical background and culture that they can and should be unapologetically proud of. Everything that was there in the past still resides in our DNA. People with our same DNA built empires; they were leaders, kings, and queens and progressed through leaps and bounds. That hope, the light that shines from every person on the planet, the hope for good and peace and harmony—all of it just needs to be acquired, owned, and groomed into something that makes a positive difference.

Every individual has the potential to make a choice, be it doing good or doing bad, following the right or wrong path. Yes, it's a matter of choice. We can bring about some good in our immediate surroundings that others at far distances can benefit from. At the same time, as many do, we can make the lives of others a living hell for ourselves and the people close to us. The choice is ours, and it always will be. The only thing that matters is what we choose to do and how we choose to do it. Many people in the world have noble intentions, and yet they go about things using poor judgment. This is unacceptable because others cannot see what is within you; they can only see your actions, so you need to ensure that your work accurately reflects your intentions.

If you claim to be a sane person who prioritizes peace but goes around picking fights, you might be able to justify it to yourself somehow, but you're unlikely to convince others. You cannot preach peace and equality while simultaneously making a habit of practicing racial hate. No matter our social standing or position in life, we deserve fairness and should be judged based on our character.

As for me, I choose not to impose on others or crowd their space. But my sentiment aligns with Christopher Woods when a reason to fight is unavoidable:

"I will fight like I am one of three monkeys on the ramp to Noah's Ark, and brother, it's starting to rain."

CHAPTER 4

Government Executive

There were instances when I seriously wanted to quit, particularly whenever I was dealing with evil minds with limited mental capacity. The human souls in my life who inspired me in times of such challenges were my cousin Adam, my best friend, James Wilson, and later my wife, Aracely.

As always, I frequently had private conversations with my God. That kind of closeness enabled me to look at discouragement with a smile and acknowledge that giving up isn't in my DNA. Through it all, I learned to focus less on limiting my challenges and more on challenging my limits. I learned earlier in life that through such struggles, I gained more insight into what was happening and recognized that opportunities are often disguised as challenges.

Even when I thought about quitting, God reminded me to be true to myself. I knew then that the real option was to tread ahead, knowing that succeeding or failing was up to me no matter what. And even if I fail, at least what I learned from the experience provided me insight into a path yet to be traveled.

For me, anything that is attained with hard and smart work is worth it. I value my achievements a lot. Maybe what I was trying to do just wasn't meant for me to accomplish at the time. Even so, I would have learned valuable lessons in the attempt, lessons that will serve me in other areas of my life.

I have always chosen diligence in my ventures and recognized that being performance-driven and outcome-focused has its benefits.

I had a successful career in the hotel industry for 16 years at the senior level. For 25 years, I was a senior grade staff member for the U.S. Army Community and Family Support Center (USACFSC), a DoD agency. Following retirement from CFSC, I served nine years in higher education as an Adjunct College Professor at Prince George's Community College. I subsequently left Prince George's Community College and moved to Graduate School, USA a subsidiary of American Public Education, Inc. American Public University System | Rasmussen University | as a senior instructor. Along with my teaching career, which is still active, I continued as an entrepreneur and Chief Operating Officer (COO) for Turning Point Coaching, LLC, a successfulconsulting, coaching, training, and professional development firm.

I served briefly in the Army but was issued a physical disability-honorable discharge due to an injury during basic training. I never thought the opportunity to serve again would cross my path. My return to the military, even though it was by way of DoD as a civilian, was quite an honor.

Being an individual who took whatever comes my way in stride, it very fulfilling when I was offered the opportunity to work for the militar. I knew I could handle the challenges that could come with working for the CFSC. For instance, being sent on assignments across the globe where 75 percent of my work assignments required travel with me having little to no say in where I was going could have posed some concerns, but I didn't let it bother me. Also, I never knew how dangerous an assignment might turn out to be, though that possibility was remote. On the positive side, traveling the world was full of adventures. After all, aren't we all frustrated with life's boring and humdrum routine of staying at one point or another?

I mentioned before that I was seriously injured in a car crash, went through several surgical procedures because of the accident, and that my chances of walking again were slim to none. However, with my faith in God, the help, and support of my family, and sheer willpower, I didn't just walk, I was able to run. Nonetheless, based on my injury, following recovery and subsequent injury while in basic training, I was considered physically ineligible for the battlefield and given an honorable physical disability discharge from the Army. I was quite heartbroken since I had been discharged, I had committed myself to continue my career in the Army, but due to someone else's irresponsible and drunk driving, I missed that once-in-a-lifetime opportunity.

I was challenged to contain my emotions when. several years later, I was recruited to work for the military. My emotions stemmed from thinking my chance to serve was long gone. The fact that I was, here and now, given a second chance by being selected to serve those who served our country was worth and even greater than any opportunity I could imagine. The offer I initially accepted entailed operating a hotel affiliated with the U.S. Army in Seoul, South Korea. However, when the time came for me to go to Korea, my assignment with orders were abruptly shifted to what was then West Germany.

It was explained to me during my interview that the U.S. Department of Defense mandated that every military installation have a non-appropriated funds (NAF) program.

And that, instituting the NAF program was a strategy to integrate and support Family and Morale, Welfare and Recreation programs and services, enabling readiness and resilience for a globally responsive Army. The NAF programs included a diverse grouping of self-sufficient business operations on U.S. Military Installations worldwide, the grouping of self-sufficient business operations programs functioning under Morale, Welfare, and Recreation (MWR). The NAF and MWR programs provided for and supported military personnel through Rest and Relaxation (R&R): R&R, and other purposes. The NAF MWR programs also supported and served military families, so they could enjoy the same experiences that they did back home, in the U.S., while accompanying their spouse overseas. The non-appropriated funds were those funds generated by self-sufficient revenue producing business programs. (E.g., hotels, clubs and restaurants, golf, bowling, etc.). Meaning the program operations and services provided aren't paid for by tax dollars.

Only authorized personnel are allowed to use or stay in these establishments, including civilians, as long as they are authorized by the Department of Defense (DoD), including personnel who are traveling on government assignments. These employees, who were on official travel, were given the option to stay in facilities outside the base's gate or in facilities inside the base's gate, provided it did not interfere with their mission.

My first assignment took me to the U.S. Army Community and Family Support Center (USACFSC) European Regional Office (USACFSC ERO). It entailed working as a team leader focused on coaching, advising, and training civilian and uniform personnel on Military Installations. The scope of my assignment was much broader than managing a hotel. I traveled throughout Europe, the Middle East, parts of Africa, and the Pacific Rim, coaching, advising, and training Department of Defense (DoD) personnel on Military Installations.

I must admit, while I was enthusiastic about the broad assignments, I was partial to hotel management. As such, I approached the office's executive officer (XO), Major Nelson, who reported to the director, Colonel Lew Turner, early in my assignment. I wanted to know what the chances were that I would operate a hotel during my service working with CFSC, reiterating that I was initially recruited to operate a hotel.

The major told me point-blank that it was very unlikely I would be assigned to a hotel. For some reason, I took his response personally. While I didn't observe anything out of character with the major's demeanor, as he was always abrupt, I was surprised and disappointed with how he spoke to me. I later approached the Director, Colonel Lew Turner, directly and was given the same answer, albeit even more rudely. I persisted, asking the director why he wouldn't even consider assigning me a hotel to manage, and the director just looked at me with his eyes reflecting racial scorn and said, "No, absolutely not!"

Having been recruited to operate a hotel, bringing 16 productive and successful years in hospitality management with me, I was mystified by leadership's refusal to give me an opportunity for a hotel assignment and refusing to do so with such contempt.

My meeting with Col. Turner, the Director, happened a couple of days after the meeting with Major Nelson, the XO. I didn't know if the Executive Officer had told the Director what I had asked him. However, the fact that I wasn't going to be considered to operate a hotel was made certain in no uncertain terms. Not being one to let anything derail my focus, I decided to get on with my assignments. Not long afterward, I realized that the opportunity was, in some ways, better than just operating a hotel, and I became more excited. This mission meant helping leaders who would go on to manage various operations, including hotels on and off military installations.

I was coaching, advising, and training others on the skills that I learned, including strategic and business planning, motivation and customer service, food and beverage management, financial management and budgeting, and many other skills. This opportunity was very motivating for me. It was an opportunity to take others under my wing, just as Peter Schruender, my mentor, once took me under his wing. The fact is that technical assistance, coaching, advising, and training the masses made me proud, knowing the effect that a good teacher can have on the lives of others.

While working on my current assignment, Col. Turner, the Director, completed his tour of duty and was replaced by his Deputy, Lt. Col. Pete Issacs. I had been refused an appointment to a hotel assignment before for some unknown reason that only my director and maybe others around him understood, including Lt. Col. Issacs.

When I took the matter up with my new Director, Lt. Col. Pete Issacs, I was told, with some politeness, that "it's a thought worth considering, but not right now." The "it's a thought worth considering" never came to pass. Lt. Col. Isaacs never, to my knowledge, acted on appointing me the General Manager of any of the many military-operated hotels. My intuition strongly led me to believe it was a racial issue, which would explain why the offer never came to pass. No one in the system had the level of competence, in terms of education, specialty training, and experience, in hospitality management as I did, despite some having a military club, food and beverage background at the time of their hotel assignment, except one who had a degree in hospitality management. But they did have one thing in common; they were all white males.

Even though I was never assigned as a General Manager, Hotel Operations, the position I was originally hired for, I did very well during my career with the U.S. Army CFSC. I decided, since the USA CFSC ERO's leadership was not going to offer me the position I was initially interviewed and hired for (General Manager, Hotel Operations), I might as well make the best of a good situation.

I worked with many teams, and depending on the assignment, I was often the team leader. Particularly if the mission was training and professional development, focusing more on how to improve customer service, sanitation, financial management, and forecasting for the managers at the various installations, providing guidance and advice based on the particular business plans, policies, and regulations.

One notable fact is that I encountered more racial bias during my career working for the U.S. Army CFSC than I did while working in the private sector hotel industry. When I took the matter up with myaThe main difference between my hotel industry discrimination in the private sector versus the U.S. Army CFSC military variety was that in the private sector, discrimination was overt and came from the public (customers), but I had strong support from my leadership. new Director, Lt. Col. Pete Issacs, I was told, with some politeness, that "it's a thought worth considering, but not right now." In the U.S. Army CFSC, however, discrimination came from supervisors and senior leadership, not the uniform personnel, family members, and civilians we served.

Discrimination among leadership was subtle and covert but pointed and easily recognizable. I was never passed over for promotions, nor was my pay ever docked. Nevertheless, I would face random unnecessary racial issues regularly. I always refused to allow others' stupidity, regardless of rank or grade, to derail my focus. For example, I saw an opportunity as the first civilian member from the CFSC HQs' office, recruited to attend the Military Installation Leadership and Management Program at the U.S. Army Management Staff College (USAMSC), Fort Belvoir, Virginia, and jumped on it.

I completed a 90–day intensive and extensive Military Leadership and Management Development Program. Then I submitted my graduation certificate and transcript to the American Council on Education (ACE), resulting in an equivalent of 15 credit hours toward a master's degree. I parlayed those 15 credits into earning a second Master of Science degree, this one in Military Installation Management from the University of Maryland University College.

I took the opportunity of the Leadership and Management Development Program as a research project assignment to prove or disprove my suspicion of structural racism within the U.S. Army Community and Family Support Center (USACFSC). I did so in a white paper where I collected the necessary data and conducted an analysis of who, based on race, the leadership of the U.S. Army Community and Family Support Center (USACFSC), placed in various positions based on what factors and submitted it as my assignment. I could have been satisfied by that since I was recruited at a senior-level pay grade; however, that wasn't enough for me. There were several other promising individuals, African Americans like me, who should have moved up the ladder and made major contributions to the system as well.

Several white fellow employees suggested that it was just my personal belief. So, I chose to use the researched white paper to prove or disprove that assertion. The research proved that my point of view was right. I used USACFSC data and other public documents to support my position.

Also, the office would show, during all-hands-on-deck meetings, video footage of military activity and installations in Iraq, Saudi Arabia, and other Middle Eastern countries.

All of the military personnel (Officers and enlisted) in those videos were white. Anyone who viewed those videos could reasonably conclude that only white leaders and white soldiers were fighting in Dessert Storm.

I decided to take this up with CFSC's leadership, pointing out that black people should be shown fighting for their country too. The ratio of whites to blacks in the overseas installations was about 70-to-30, and yet there wasn't any representation of black soldiers in those videos. Why? An answer was never provided.

When I was reviewing an MWR video that belonged to the Military Installation Club system, a huge Confederate flag was displayed on the wall in the background, and a singer playing and singing country music was shown in the video. The MWR Business Academy leadership, whether intentionally or naïvely, directed me to include the video in a training tour at various military installations I was leading. Of course, with the video including the confederate flag on the wall, I decided against including it in any of my training.

My boss was somewhat irked by my decision, but that video would not be included as long as I was in charge of delivering the training. I refused to conduct training that included a video with the rebel flag as its centerpiece on Military Installations. And I made that decision with the clarity of mind that it was okay with me if the leadership decided to terminate me.

Right at the beginning of my hotel management career, I decided that staying open-minded and sticking to principles was my path to survival.

I was raised to show respect and treat people with dignity while holding my head high and accepting nothing less. That mindset got me through having to contend with the fire of racial hatred, bigotry, and other falsely projected feelings of privilege. Those who stuck to the traditional ideas that white privilege was everything were often amazed when I treated them with respect while consistently being unapologetically black, proud, and dignified.

I firmly believe that open-mindedness is a strength, and anyone in a leadership position can benefit from that strength when they recognize and respect their personnel from different social and cultural backgrounds. They should respect and own it with grace.

These issues may not seem very important to some. However, the absence of treating people with dignity and respect serve as void for bigotry's building blocks. Some people grow up feeling entitled because they are taught from an early age that they are the superior race, only to find that, when working together, the whole is greater than the sum of its parts. And a superior race mentality does not provide for a full return on investment.

I continue to align with the belief:

"Nothing in the entire world is more dangerous than sincere ignorance and conscientious stupidity."

-Martin Luther King, Jr.

When telling Ms. Cheryl Mbaye, also a former USA CFSC employee, that I was writing my memoir, she asked if I plan to include my USA CFSC career? When I said yes, she offered to provide a minor contribution about the USA CFSC's work environment.

I was receptive to her offer, and her comments follow: "Derk, for your consideration, focusing solely on my experience, please make my comments that follow a part of your book, "Was I Your First?": Progression of America's First African-American General Manager for a Major Brand Hotel in USA History. Starting with the trending dissonance spawned by politicians fanning racial flames all while being tone deaf to the many inequities faced by the Black community has been extremely disappointing to me, causing me to reflect upon my career in the military, non-appropriated (NAF), and appropriated (APF) fund jobs. I must admit that I was a bit naïve in believing that opportunities have improved for Blacks in the workplace and in certain ways they have but at times, it seems as if any gains made are being chipped away and eroded faster than they appeared. Using myself as an example, I have personally experienced and witnessed everything from microaggression to outright racism in the workplace. Overall, my experience has been marked by having to work twice as hard and twice as smart as my white counterpart to get the job, get the job done and still without getting the credit. The most personally hurtful experience I have had; however, was my employment with US Army Community and Family Support Center (USACFSC) where I served in a support role as Chief, Hospitality Support. I generally enjoyed fulfilling my job responsibilities which included "serving soldiers and their families" by providing liaison between Headquarters (located in Alexandria, VA) and four resort hotels (Armed Forces Recreation Centers, AFRCs) with locations in Germany, Korea, Hawaii, and Orlando) and a slot machine operation with locations in Germany, Korea and Japan (Army Recreation Machine Program).

I had what I would call a decent career with Army MWR and worked my way up from a Secretary to Program Analyst (1984-2008); all the while not realizing that I had an unstated benefactor (the Chief Operating Officer, "COO") who offered me some level of protection within the organization until such time that he sadly became ill and announced his retirement). I admired the COO, and he was well respected within and outside of the organization. As soon as he announced his retirement, however, I was fair game with a target on my head when plans for a reorganization emerged. In fact, it was at a General Manager's Off-Site meeting at the Shades of Green (Orlando,

FL) where the COO officially announced his retirement and it was announced that a new position, "Chief of Hospitality" had been created with greater responsibilities (to which the incumbent Chief of Army Lodging was assigned). The incumbent Director of Hospitality with whom I worked (and who would later become the Chief Operating Officer) had not even had the decency to inform me of organizational changes directly impacting me. In fact, I learned of the organizational change during the meeting and could barely contain my shock as I endured the meeting and subsequent return to work. I am grateful that in eventually discussing my situation with Derk Mattocks, he was able to provide counsel and encouragement that subsequently led me to move on from Army MWR. I am also grateful that I was able to work in the interim with NAF Contracting until such time as I was able to leave USACFSC altogether. My later work experience leading up to my eventual retirement was favorably impacted by my Army MWR experience. Having developed enviable skill sets over the years, I was able to use said skills and was greatly appreciated in my later jobs and for that I am thankful. Derk Mattocks is someone whom I have known professionally since 1984 in Europe, when I joined USACFSC, European Regional Office (ERO) freshly out of the Air Force. I have greatly admired how he commanded respect and how he managed to not tolerate attempts to treat him unequally in the workplace. For that, I appreciate and am happy that he welcomes my input into his book. Overall, I am grateful for my experiences and opportunities with Army MWR and the wonderful people I have met along the way, but the way it ended, cloaked is systemic racism, for me remains a bitter disappointment. Thankfully to Mr. Mattocks, I was able to move on to another agency, excel, and never looked back.

CHAPTER 5

Government Executive

I used to work as General Manager of hotel, food, and beverage operations for a couple of world-class hotels before being recruited by the U.S. Army Community and Family Support Center (USACFSC). However, the Army wasn't the only armed forces branch I worked with. When I joined the agency, USACFSC provided technical assistance (coaching, training, supervisory, and leadership development) for executives charged with operating businesses and programs on Military Installations worldwide. These Military Installations, while primarily Army, also included the Marine Corps and the Air Force.

I coached, advised, and trained many of these military and civilian staff members. The classes I taught were not limited to food and beverage services, customer services, financial management, and analysis, marketing, and supervisory and leadership development. Many of the courses were taught at the MWR Business Academy at the USACFSC headquarters in Falls Church, Virginia. I also led a team of professionals who traveled to Military Installations worldwide, coaching and training MWR personnel and leadership, as mentioned previously. The job's toughest yet most fun part was the "technical assistance" element, which involved hands-on work and training. This was real-time management of people who, often times, had minimal training to do jobs that required a great deal of training and experience.

All businesses and related programs were operated as self-sustaining non-appropriated funds. None of the costs incurred, including the salaries of the civilian personnel, were passed on to the taxpayers.

Serving as a technical assistance expert, I advised on business and marketing planning, trend analysis and forecasting, etc. My advice and follow-through ensured that the products and services management provided met the standards as prescribed by the AR 215 (agency policy).

Most of the guests at these establishments were uniform personnel, their families, and civilian personnel working there or on government travel orders. The goal was to make sure that these guests were well taken care of.

The essential skillset I tried to inspire was that of servant management and leadership mindset. To do so, I drew on my education, experience, and positive mindset and went deep into my tools set, emphasizing active listening, critical thinking, and problem-solving associated with whatever coaching or training I conducted. I would frame each curriculum into teaching the aspects most suited to a particular role.

For example, if I were teaching a class of managers, I would ensure that they were learning all of the minutiae of running a hotel, couched in confidence, competence, and courage. If I were teaching a class of supervisors, I would teach them the sorts of insights they needed to know to give the level of service one would expect from a professional business operation. Managers also needed to know how to develop monthly and annual budgets to manage the business to profitability.

Non-appropriated fund (NAF) operations were required to turn a profit or break even to sustain the business. However, I refused to recommend cutting corners or shortchanging the customer.

I practiced what I preached by drawing on my listening, critical thinking, and problem-solving skills, putting my education and experience in management and leadership to good use. I also earned certification in strategic thinking, and all of the knowledge and experience I accumulated over the years helped me simplify some of the complex issues. I understood management well, and my command of its nuances enabled me to teach the essentials to anyone with maximum impact.

My entire career with the U.S. Army Community and Family Support Center (USACFSC) was based less on teaching everything I knew and more on teaching what my students/clients needed to know to succeed in their respective scope of responsibilities. I often talk to people first, to get a better understanding of what their needs are. If it were a group, I would conduct surveys. From these conversations, I would discover their strengths and weaknesses.

This approach helped sustain my career as a coach, trainer, and advisor with the agency for twenty-five years. I always believed that I could communicate the core concepts of management and processes to just about anyone because I learned about the individuals before I started teaching them. I knew who I was dealing with and the best teaching methods for them. On top of that, I always approached with an open mind and treated everyone, from senior management to the rank and file, with dignity, respect, and compassion. There is great value in treating people with dignity, respect, and compassion. It enables me to create an atmosphere conducive to learning.

I stressed the value of humility while interacting with all students/clients, regardless of grade or rank; I would never pretend to know their business better than those in charge of their operation. I often lauded their ingenuity in various aspects of their work. Whenever I was stuck and didn't understand something, I would seek and find the answer(s), then use that insight to enhance my professional abilities further and share it with others.

The only thing that mattered to me was ensuring that the customers were satisfied and that I had done everything possible to ensure that outcome.

I often came across plenty of people who may or may not have wished me well; however, they did show respect to me because of my behavior, professionalism, strong performance, and commitment. At every installation I visited, I connected with the senior leadership of the installation and, subsequently, with rank-and-file workers. A courteous nature with confidence can get people's attention and help win friends and allies.

Since retirement, I have even received several offers from people in senior management whom I worked with who themselves are now retired and working in the government or who are now in the private sector.

Whenever I talk about how much I have done and achieved in my life and how many stereotypes, stigmas, and racists I had to overcome to get to where I am, I must always give credit to Belgrade, my hometown.

Belgrade was the foundation upon which everything within my core was built. It wasn't just books and schools; it was much more. Children in Belgrade were taught a way of life. We were taught that we could excel, and be anything we wanted to be, and if we didn't excel, we could be good; if not good, we could be kind, and anyone can be kind. It's a matter of choice.

One of my biggest achievements was being recruited in 1968 and excelling as the first African American hotel manager on the white side of town; continuing 16 years through 1984, at a time when discrimination against black people was at an all-time high, hidden under a white sheet and hood, during a time when the country was reeling from the "phasing out" of segregation. Less we forget: When I say "phasing out" of segregation, I am speaking of a historic sociological problem - Racial segregation hidden under a white sheet and hood is transitioning to a suit and tie, seated in high places throughout institutions, including the governments, for the practice of limiting black people to certain circumscribed areas of residence or to separate institutions (e.g., schools, churches) and facilities (parks, playgrounds, restaurants, restrooms) based on race. Racial segregation provided a means of maintaining the economic advantages and superior social status to the benefit and privilege of white populations to maintain their ascendancy over other groups through legal and social color bars.

I refused to be deterred; I lived my life managing hotels based on a simple philosophy. I didn't disrespect anyone or allow anyone to disrespect me. Even though it sometimes irked some of my senior leadership, I maintained a straightforward and unapologetic attitude not to accept the racist notion that I was not every bit as valuable as any white man who came before me. That resilience and insistence on being seen as an equal made me stand out. Some said that I was cherry-picked from among the many people whom I worked with, which might speak to my character.

My parents and the people of Belgrade were role models that I looked up to. The humility that comes from being surrounded by so many good people during my childhood influenced me greatly. It wasn't as if I chose one person and decided that I was going to model myself after that particular person. I knew from an early age that everyone has good qualities and that the way to progress in life is to be prepared to learn from everyone.

I sometimes came across individuals whom I was responsible for coaching, training, or advising but who were not motivated to listen and participate just because of my color. Rather than create an antagonist environment, I realized that was my chance to be a role model for those who were going to be dealing with customers long after I was gone. I inspired them to work, no matter how menial or complex the task was. I looked for ways to get through to them, and eventually, it worked.

It never mattered to me what the person's station was. All that mattered was that the outcomes were very positive when I treated them with dignity, respect, and compassion and held them accountable to treat me likewise. This was because I met some people who would not have treated me with respect if they had had the choice.

I was always conscious of walking a fine line when conducting myself for business. While recognizing and respecting that my leadership's scope of responsibilities is greater than mine, I never viewed anyone as superior. As mentioned before, I would not countenance disrespect from anyone, nor would I disrespect anyone. Nonetheless, I did report to a few, from time to time, whom I believe would have insulted me the first chance they got had I not conducted myself the way that I did. And yes, some of the suspects were senior leaders in uniform.

While this might sound confusing, there's a difference between being rude and standing your ground with strength, kindness, humility, and pride. I just chose not to be a pushover at someone else's perceived privilege expense. That's something most people these days just don't understand. They think that to assert dominance or gain control of a situation, one must be physically imposing loud, or abrasive in some way.

My life's experience has proved to me that nothing could be furthest from the truth, and I am a living example. I always taught my two daughters, that, more often than not, there are better ways to gain control of a situation through calm, cool, and peaceful means A lesson I learned from my mother. Of course, there were times when that method may not prove fruitful, and the situation may get out of hand. Even in those situations, I was never rude and rarely, if ever, raised my voice. I would just offer the other side options and even be open to accepting options from the other side as long as it did not degrade anyone. I always assessed leverage, determined my wiggle room, and worked from that perspective.

I firmly believe that a person's behavior reflects their character. My learning and education starting at Belgrade and Silverdale were central to my character, and my education and experiences at Georgetown High can best be summed up by the word "holistic" but deep. It was a combination of the education and nurturing that I received in elementary through high school, along with a healthy dose of reality for what was in store for me, that set me on a path and commitment to excel. It was an eye-opening experience for me to go through Georgetown as the experience painted a realistic picture of the real world instead of the cultural bubble in which I had always been protected.

CHAPTER 6

Serving In Higher Education

My experience working for USACFSC, servicing and supporting the military, was a productive and energized one, filled with learnings, contributions, adventures, disruptions, and some contentment. Even though I had left the Army, against my wishes, with an honorable discharge with a disability, all those years before, I did not blame the government; my injuries before I was drafted and later during basic training made me physically challenged to continue in the military service. It was almost poetic, as if somehow, I ended up serving for 25 years, although not in the way I had envisioned originally.

I felt a strange sense of peace within the military environment. It felt as though I had achieved something very significant. As a senior grade level career DoD civilian, I went, I saw, I did, and I was pleased with the outcome. I traveled throughout the (Pacific Rim, the Middle East, Europe, parts of Africa, and the United States) world serving and helping make a positive impact on and for those in uniform who served and their families.

I never thought, for once, that my service to the military was any less significant than my service in managing major brand hotels. All of it holds a special place in my heart. Even though I faced a whirlwind of racial challenges from some among my leadership, I still felt proud to serve and support those in uniform, often in harm's way, defending our lifestyle in the United States of America. That was very important to me. It was truly my pride and joy.

I was always mused about how odd it was that a Department of the Army agency, Within the Department of Defense sought me out to serve as a senior-level civilian. It was as if fate had led them to me so that I could find closure. When it was time to retire as a civilian, I was far from finished following my years with the military. Yes, while I did retire, God was positioning me to reinvent myself. I have always believed that a person should stay moving and active, and I took that very seriously. With that mindset, my wife Aracely and I decided to make our home in Maryland. Considering that my wife's relatives are a four-hour drive north and my relatives are a four-hour drive south. We felt Maryland was ideal for building our home. Hence, in Maryland, it was.

There, following retiring, with God's help, I prepared myself for refiring. Since leading, training, and developing others had always been a huge part of my life, I reinvented myself, energized my passion connected with my knowledge, education, and experiences, presented myself, and was accepted as an Adjunct Professor at Prince George's Community College.

Since I held an MSc, Mgmt., and an MBA, I was asked to teach business studies and economics. I started teaching at Prince George's Community College in 2009 and taught there for the better part of a decade until 2019. Teaching was much more than simply communicating to students what I had learned and passing knowledge on to them. I was more committed to paying it forward, establishing a legacy where I help others, open up their mind, treat others with dignity and respect, and contribute to society. I was committed to going to any length of reasoning to reach each student and motivate them to have a progressive mindset and be confident in one's self while owning their vision; to be committed to its purpose; to build competence through learning, creativity, and how to be resourceful; recognizing that they have the necessary solutions within. For me, teaching meant taking students under my wing, serving as a mentor, and creating a trusting environment conducive to learning.

I refused to underestimate the significance of the role of a teacher in a student's life. After all, I had some of my teachers to model myself after. I often found similarities between my childhood classroom and the ones I taught in. Yes, some students were there just to be there, but I was committed to ensuring they left knowing more, feeling better, and more positive than when they came. I connected with many and mentored some to refocus and get their lives on track. I even helped some get started in their respective careers.

Likewise, there were students whom I was able to convince to seek higher degrees. Some of whom still keep in touch. They continue to reach out to me to tell me what they are up to. And trust me when I say students staying in touch with me is a source of high energy, great pride, and satisfaction for me. The fact that my students trusted my judgment and counsel went a long way to establishing my legacy. The knowledge I imparted to them, both academically and by facilitating questions regarding their personal lives and having them find their solutions, created strong bonds. I proudly encouraged my students to pay it forward in their respective communities, sharing their open-minded approach and insights with others. And hopefully, they would forward it again and again. That's my legacy.

During my time at Prince George's Community College, an opportunity became available for me to teach overseas. The dean of my department considered my skillset and vast experience traveling during my time with the Department of Defense (DoD) and recommended me for the opportunity. Even though I was unable to accept the assignment, I found the dean's words very touching. I knew that the dean of business meant every single word, as her dedication to her job and passion were very apparent.

I was always committed to managing and keeping my priorities straight. I knew that my days of traveling, as extensive as I did with DoD, were behind me. And that it was important from a mental, physical, emotional, and motivational standpoint that I returned home after such a long and successful career and continued to contribute to society in my community.

Coming back and working in my new community was very important for me. I always needed to focus and do something with my time, for I could never be content being retired and doing nothing. After all, I had traveled much of the world several times over, so traveling was not a great motivator. At a minimum, I kept a grueling exercise routine that I learned during my injury that became a habit.

Teaching at a community college was an experience for me. An experience that I felt couldn't be substituted with being at a four-year university. At the community college, I dealt with people who had interrupted their educations early in their lives to make money or start families, many returning on a shoestring and a prayer. Most of my students were twenty-five, thirty years, and older, and their early school days were mostly long past. As a result, I found them motivated to achieve their goals.

Something I think I saw about adults who attend community college is that they have the desire but may have lost their focus, and that's what I helped with. Yes, there were guidance counselors, but I took the time and was proud of the fact that I was teaching people who realized that they had responsibilities and were trying to own up to those responsibilities.

Many of my students were single parents who had to go through some challenges just to get to school and take classes. Their dedication made my choice easy. I realized that I needed to stay and create an atmosphere for them that was motivational, inspirational, and conducive to learning. That's what drove me and what continues to drive me to this day. My teaching and developmental strategies were framed to ensure that all of my students, regardless of the subject, were motivated to give their all in all their classes.

That "all" meant having them consider critical thinking a universal domain-general thinking skill. It means that no matter what path or profession any one of them pursues, critical thinking is a skill that can help get them through the process. I wanted my students to know that they would want to make conscious choices if they wanted to live their best, most successful, and happy lives. And making those conscious choices can be done with a simple process known as critical thinking. Critical Thinking was good enough for Socrates, and it is good enough for any student in my class.

I was committed to using exercises in classes that encouraged critical thinking and questions, having students recognize the benefits of critical thinking. Likewise, I incorporated the tapestry of active listening, promoted its values, encouraged its practice, and held students accountable for responsive and responsible responses.

With advances in technology, it's become very easy to obtain information. The assignments I gave out made use of information easily available on the Internet. However, I always urged students that whenever they read up on any assignment, be open to listening to their peers for new insight, if for nothing more than a different perspective, to include someone who's just giving their opinion. I encouraged students, as an audience, when listening, to listen actively. Listening actively enables a person to give respect to the speaker and discern the value of the speaker's content, message, and level of insight the speaker has in whatever they are talking about.

Like critical thinking, active listening requires the listener to fully concentrate, understand, respond, and then remember what is being said. Like critical thinking, active listeners make a conscious effort to hear and understand the complete message being spoken rather than just passively hearing the message of the speaker.

However, one might say that I was a stickler for materials that had been peer-reviewed. While I accept that books might be outdated, I believe many of the principles in these books still hold value. Whenever I am in teaching mode and observing a student who thinks they have all the answers, I politely but briefly hand over the class to them until they recognize their shortcomings and revert to the receiving and discussion process. I recognize and easily acknowledge that everyone has a point of view. I rarely give out the answer; rather, I guide them on how they can find the answer for themselves.

Even though I prefer using peer-reviewed work and textbooks for teaching, I encourage the younger generation to consult the Internet for help with their assignments. I encourage them to research, prove or disprove their inquiry, and think their way through the assignments to develop their minds while thinking through critical situations.

Many of my students found themselves transiting from the mindset of "We have always done it this way" to exploring the question of "What if?" often coming up with new approaches on their own. I often found myself gaining insight from their perspective.

Taking my classes on field trips and inviting successful business owners and other organization leaders to come to my classes and give talks prove most beneficial. Students can take greater advantage of this because they are given an environment where their minds are shaped to think critically as other professionals in their respective fields do.

The projects assigned are always targeted toward a better understanding of the subject matter. Because I take my job seriously, I assign tasks with a purpose. And I find it therapeutic going through each assignment, focusing on outcomes framed best for what the student should learn and understand, rather than simply parroting what is written in the textbook.

I would submit that life is rarely going to be what textbooks teach. Even if a concept that needs to be applied in a practical situation is shown in a textbook, chances are that it will still need to be modified to fit the situation. Real-life challenges rarely have textbook answers, and that's why critical and creative thinking are so important.

I can recall one particular student, a young lady, who was very argumentative. No matter the subject, she would take an opposing view for no other reason than to be overtly contrary. I welcomed debates, but that was not her purpose. The young lady would take issue when the class was discussing topics with supporting facts at hand, setting goals when planning an activity, and deciding on an approach for that activity. The young lady would always elevate the focus to her opinion based on her beliefs. The other students, about twelve of them in the class, indicated discomfort being in class when she was present.

I took notice and asked her to stay back one day. I asked her if the attitude she brought to the class was the same one she had at work and home. The young lady immediately became defensive. I informed her that my question wasn't meant to judge her; But rather to help determine her validity for her reasoning.

Realizing that the discussion wasn't going to be very productive, I let it go for the time being. The young lady returned later and apologized, saying that she didn't mean to be disrespectful. I assured her that she was entitled to her perspective and, likewise, as were others. I informed her that an open mind and a respectful approach could make an atmosphere more conducive to learning. I suggested she make an appointment and come to the teacher's lounge to talk with me. I had noticed, too, that she always seemed angry about something, and when she came to the lounge, she told me that's exactly what her family thought as well. She asked if there was any way that I could help her. I told her that was not my area of expertise but that I would refer to school counseling. However, I did tell her that I would give her something to think about.

I shared with her four categories of people who can create tension and asked her to think about which one might fit her. I informed her that the first category is centered around people who, when presented with facts, become argumentative for no apparent reason. I shared with her that if she thought that was her, she should first determine whether what the person was saying was indeed factual. If it were, then she needs to show maturity, accept it, and move on.

The second category dealt with goals and objectives. If you are at home, work, or anywhere else, discuss (providing your input) and agree on something, then that's what you need to support to accomplish the outcome sought. I went on to explain that agreement, following her input, and reducing tension was in order. She agreed.

I then told her about the third category, which is about the way we do things. When you're in a work situation, the person in charge reserves the prerogative to have the final say in how things are done based on policies and procedures. You may not agree, but it's not your decision. You accepted the job and need to comply with procedures as long they're moral, ethical, and legal.

She picked up on this one quickly. I shared with her that the last category is belief. Two people can look at the same "whatever" and have different beliefs, and neither is in a better position to question the other person's beliefs with any validity. I advised her that when she was at home dealing with her family or at work dealing with fellow employees, she should think of those categories to determine the root cause of where she stood and to think about those points when she's at work and elsewhere.

She thanked me and left. Fast forward to the following week, the young lady came to class and apologized to her classmates. She told them that she was turning over a new leaf and would treat each classmate with dignity and respect. The rest of the class was touched; as a token of appreciation, they brought her a bag of cookies on the last day of class. This just shows me how far people are willing to go if you take even the smallest step toward being a better person. However, there is a bigger way to look at this.

This student was angry and argumentative without a conscious reason and did not even realize the negative impact of her behavior on others. She took seriously the conversation we had and drew on the strength and discipline necessary to come up with solutions to her challenge. Her sudden revelation or insight was so impressive that the people she saw once a week for fourteen weeks brought her a small gift in appreciation. This just goes to show that even a small step in the right direction, with friendly support, can go a long way in effecting positive change.

Later, this student shared with me that my "counseling" had helped change her outlook on life. I learned, too, that this young lady was a veteran. I thanked her for her service, we shook hands with an embrace and went our separate ways.

I tell of this experience only because of her feedback's significant impact on me. I knew, occasionally, that some in my class would fail to meet the requirements to pass the course, causing mental and emotional challenges. This particular student had a challenge that potentially threatened her success in passing the course. Hopefully, I aided her in looking within and finding a solution. This experience, one among several, motivated me to double down on my efforts to reach my students in every way possible.

Teaching was a phenomenal experience for me. Earlier in my career, I worked 16 challenging years and succeeded as a high-end hotel manager, followed by 25 years of traveling the world training, coaching, and advising both uniform and civilian DoD personnel. I retired and finally settled into teaching economics and business management at the college level. Of all my career jobs, to that point, teaching was my favorite, despite the long hours of grading papers, writing lesson plans, and keeping myself updated. I loved every minute of the experience.

CHAPTER 7

Entrepreneur

I worked and was successful in three industries, including hotel management (16 yrs.), Federal government (executive coaching, training, and professional development) (25 yrs.), and higher education (9 yrs.), for a total of 50 years. During those fifty years, I had seven employers, (Hospitality-5, Federal Gov-1 and Higher Education-1) leaving each employer at a time of my choosing and with recognition upon my departure. With each employer, I brought a mindset of humility couched in strength, kindness, and pride. I was always conscious of being confident with the absence of rudeness; kind, but in such a way that one could not mistake it as weakness; humble, without timidity; and proud, with the absence of arrogance. When I had the opportunity to teach, I was not about to change a winning formula. Yes, my teaching experience brought unexpected moments. Like any environment, communication is a two-way street. And every so often, I found students teaching me something. I would submit that it happens more often than many are willing to admit in life. Different experiences bring different insights into the same lesson. Each year I spent teaching allowed me to expand exponentially.

I taught two three credit hours (Economics, Contract Administration, and/or Business Management) courses per semester and often brought assignments home to grade. I met many students and was able to impact many lives. Teaching, for me, was an immensely positive learning and productive experience.

I don't believe there is anything more noble that a person can do than teaching. Think about the person who had the greatest impact on you. You might think of your father, mother, a teacher, or maybe even someone you met on the street. They all have one thing in common: Their relation to you has been that of a teacher, someone you may or may not have looked up to, but in any case, you learned something significant from them.

At some level, teaching is at the core of every relationship, regardless of how long or short-lived. Likewise, if you haven't had a teacher who connected with you, you are missing out. When you have a mentor to turn to, it becomes a learning experience on a different level.

During the time I taught, I facilitated relationships among students, learning and helping broaden their insights while aligning with a pathway to their goals. My focus was to help students grow by helping them build their confidence as they learn to understand their feeling of self-assurance; and competence as they gain and learn to demonstrate characteristics and skills that enable and improve their performance; and courage to realize and act on what is important and what isn't, and care less about what other people think of you and more about what you think of yourself, all while smiling because, through it all, you dare to make a conscious choice to do the right thing.

I felt proud because, in a small way, my students represented my legacy. They were my identity. Yes, I taught them, whether economics, contract administration, or business management, and their confidence, competency, and courage gained through my teaching reflected on me, and I made sure that I left every student better off than they were when coming to my class.

The cultural experience of teaching was also something that appealed to me. I dealt with a broadly diverse group of students of ages, ethnicities, and sexual orientations, with different world views and from various walks of life. Like in every other field, my students collected ideas, problems, and solutions. Each one was much more than their GPA and degree(s) earned or any position attained.

The school where I taught was a hub of diversity, and it made for an incredibly rewarding experience. Even though the college was primarily African-American, it had a broad mix of cultures, ethnicities, and generational differences.

Having spent 40-plus years in the private and government sectors combined, reinventing myself and becoming an educator, following retirement, was quite stimulating, kept me in a thought-provoking state of mind.

During this time, both my private and government sector careers, as described earlier, were saturated with bigotry perpetuated by an inept and insecure privileged-minded element of society.

To that end, I must reiterate the sustained bias I experienced during my career as a Black man as Hotel General Manager. Discrimination directed at me came from that "significant portion of the white Jim Crow population" or the white side of town who, with their racist and privileged mentality showed a disdain for sharing. However, the stealth but sustained bias I experienced during my Federal government career was more severe and impactful, as it came from both my white uniform and civilian leadership. The racial prejudice I was subjected to in my USACFSC career was a frontline bombardment of that cadre of inside privileged mentality. Even though the racial bias was covert, it was so thick you could cut it with a knife. The fact that such sustained racial bias could be so prevalent under the army's eyes, ears, and nose tested my balanced temperament and resolve.

I retired, reinvented myself, and became an educator because of my drive to help grow minds. Yes, I could and did address racial biases during those 40-plus years in the private and government sectors, but I felt I wasn't that effective on a large scale. However, I decided to go about it a bit more discreetly by incorporating perspectives into my lesson plans. I knew that racism permeated our institutions and was unlikely to go away anytime soon. All the students I taught, especially African Americans, probably understood racism and its devastation but needed to know how to deal with it proactively. And never think that it shall not be moved because of its longevity. Regardless of what courses I was teaching that semester, I encouraged my students to become well-learned, well-grounded, well-equipped, and prepared for their unique calling. And to be courageous and insightful enough to reinvent oneself, if and when it becomes necessary, at their choosing.

I knew from my experiences that instilling fear and hatred into the hearts of my students was not the way to go. I knew the importance and practical benefits of being well-learned, well-grounded, well-equipped, and prepared to be more confident, competent, and courageous. Hence, generating a positive behavior aligned with a positive outlook produced positive outcomes. These factors combined helped me be a successful hotel manager, executive coach, and trainer in my teaching career. And when I completed my teaching career part of my life, I felt as though I had achieved something special. It was important for me to be a mentor to my students, just as many of my teachers had been to me.

Many might think that after my 16-year career as a hotel manager, 25 years as a government employee, and a decade in a career as an educator, it might have been it for me. Or that three rewarding careers would be enough, and I would now look forward to enjoying (traveling, lying on the beach with my feet in the air, and sleeping) full retirement. Yet, that isn't what happened. I have always found enjoyment in purpose. To that end, I decided to add "entrepreneur" to my list of accomplishments.

When I retired, I had already traveled the world multiple times. Even after all that, though, my zest for life and the energy I had was undiminished. So, being mentally, emotionally, and physically fit, I reinvented myself and set out on a new venture, partnering with my wife, Aracely, and started a company called Turning Point Coaching LLC It was a "unique concept" we came up with, offering executive and business coaching, training, and professional development. Sounds familiar? The idea came to me back when I was with the Department of Defense, coaching and training military and civilian personnel.

A benefit of being well-learned, well-grounded, well-equipped, and prepared enables you to be sufficiently flexible to reinvent yourself as you will. Therefore confidence, competence, and courage became even closer friends. I recognized, when given it some thought, that there were plenty of potential clients in private industry, many of them veterans who were in business, executives working for businesses, and those wishing to start a business that needed coaching, business advice, and training to enhance their skills, putting them in a better position to start or expand their business. I had the credentials to provide the suite of services offered by Turning Point Coaching, LLC.

As I began getting contracts, travel demand increased. Even though I often reminisced about being in a classroom, I am still glad the company received the recognition that it has. I started the company as a sole member, LLC helping a couple of clients who liked and benefited from the services Turning Point Coaching provided. But, traveling again was not of great interest to me. I informed my clients that our time together was coming to an end and that I would work with them for another couple of months before closing down. They told me what I already knew that their businesses had reached a positive turning point since they started working with me. They were extremely grateful to have my insights into their businesses, and they were very pleased with the positive results but disappointed with me phasing out Turning Point Coaching, LLC.

Aracely, my wife, who was a Senior Executive with the Federal Government and up for retirement following 30 years of service, made a proposition. Hence, she became a partner, and Turning Point Coaching took on many businesses and clients needing our services. Again, we decided this could be an amazing venture, given our vast experience and especially our knack for connecting with people and helping them improve.

We sought after and were awarded a DoD training opportunity. Since Turning Point Coaching had grown twofold, we took on the opportunity in confidence. I began booking clients who did business at the county, city, state, and federal levels. We found that many of our small business clients were unfamiliar with the process of competing to provide services and/or products they wanted to offer to the various levels of government.

I quickly identified the challenges many of the small business clients faced: While many knew what they needed to do, too few knew how to do what they knew they needed to do. Hence, they had the skills but lacked a plan for execution and a mindset for running their businesses. So, Turning Point Coaching's purpose for intervening in their "businesses" was to assist them in putting together their thought processes, understanding their capabilities, and how they could best present and deliver the products and/or services they offered.

Many Turning Point Coaching clients themselves could have handled all of these processes, but there was a gap that they had trouble getting past, involving their inability to identify and reach government opportunities.

I understood well the Request for Information (RFI), Request for Quotes (RFQ), and Request for Proposal (RFP) process and coached and trained some as individuals and others as a group.

Various government entity programs advertised requests for private businesses, including small businesses, to make proposals that met their products and/or service specifications. Many of the small businesses I contacted didn't know how to respond or lacked the resources.

We saw this gap and decided to become a bridge in between. Turning Point Coaching provided training, assistance, and coaching and developed proposals as appropriate. The best part about the services Turning Point Coaching provides is that we help clients without gouging them. When writing proposals, we didn't just do it because the client seeks to hire Turning Point Coaching to do it and charge a fee. For a minimum fee, we first assessed whether the client and the project were a good fit. Even if they have the skills, but chances of them getting the opportunity might be minimal; We advise them of the same, and they decide if they wish to move forward with the process, including the fee. Therefore, our logic was simple: While we cannot guarantee one way or the other, why should the client pay $2,500 or $3,000, or even more, to write a proposal when the chances of getting the project are potentially nil? Again, the client reserves the right to have the last word.

We accept a nominal fee, do an investigative analysis, and provide feedback to the client on the statistical probability of getting the contract. We let the client know up front that our method isn't foolproof but can give them some confidence when deciding to hold off or go for it. If they choose to move forward, we will assemble the proposal as appropriate. The reason for investigative analysis gives clients the real pros and cons of getting the project as either the prime contractor, seeking a subcontractor role, or passing it by.

The federal, state and local government offers various certifications to boost opportunities for veterans, minorities, women, and/or disabled veteran business owners. To be eligible to apply for respective certification (s), all applicants must, at a minimum, meet the 51 percent ownership of the business standard. While the application process is free to the applicant, with help from the respective agency, many applicants still turn to Turning Point Coaching for assistance. Aracely and I learned early when setting up Turning Point Coaching, LLC, that many eligible small business owners were unaware of the various certifications, benefits, and opportunities for minority business inclusion associated with these certifications.

Minority Business Enterprises (MBE) are typically certified by a municipality, state, or federal entity. The National Minority Supplier Development Council can add value to minority business ventures.

While some members may be able to self-identify, self-identifying does not lead to official certification and lacks making basics in the minority business inclusion arena.

Among these many programs is a certification at the federal level, known as the GSA schedule, also known as Multiple Award Schedules (MAS). The program is the federal government's premier contracting program for commercial products and services. Essentially, it's a program for the government wherein, once a client is certified to be under the GSA schedule, government agency contractors who buy for the government simply pull the catalog, which has the company's name and the company prices on it. The government representative may skip the Request for Proposal (RFP) process and call the company directly to provide the required product or services. Again, the process and certification are free of charge, but the process can be intensive and time-consuming. So, clients who are interested in applying often turn to a third party to help maneuver the process. Turning Point Coaching helps companies work through the process based on the company's capacity to qualify.

Given the quality of services provided, Turning Point Coaching's business has grown exponentially, with many of the same clients we had at the beginning.

Turning Point Coaching's growth speaks volumes about what I set out to do at the beginning of the TPC venture. That is, to reinvent myself, apply my skills, training, advising, and coaching, as appropriate, in an area of small minority business owners, working with minorities who all already had the confidence, competence, and courage to be successful but for the system to continue, heavy foot planted in their way. Reinventing myself, and starting the business, has been a blessing for me. While starting the business was largely a matter of my unwillingness to sit idly at home, I've realized that it's much more than that now. Turning Point Coaching is in a unique position to help people who otherwise might be taken advantage of. I've noticed that some businesses specializing in writing proposals charge excessive fees, and clients can do nothing about it. It ends up holding them back, and it's difficult for them to find anyone willing to do good work for a reasonable fee.

When I realized this, I didn't think there was an opportunity to make a sustainable income by keeping Turning Point Coaching prices reasonable and generating business proposals that work. But I genuinely wanted to help businesses grow, and the best way to do that would be to put my years of experience to help these small business owners at a fair and reasonable price.

One thing I believe is unique about me is that I never allowed money to be the driving force behind my decisions. I have always considered myself to be a prudent man. The fact that I can and have made "sensible decisions" throughout my life is something I am very thankful for. Reinventing myself for the business, driven by a laser-focused vision for helping minorities grow their small businesses, is rewarding. It is very inspiring to recognize many of the companies I deal with are using me as a source of knowledge to help them learn, develop, and grow. Quite frankly, I will always be proud of that. It helped me establish and sustain Turning Point Coaching's credibility.

My daughter who wrote the first version of this book, would ask me about the "secret" to my success. I would say, "struggle, infinite hard work, smart work, and luck." While she appreciated my response, she insisted on a more reasonable answer. A deep-down reflection of myself made me realize that my ability to reinvent myself multiple times over the years had a pattern that was always the same: my upbringing and the Belgrade mentality. That was where I learned crucial things, such as understanding and appreciating the value of:

- Diligence.
- Critical and creative thinking.
- Treating people with dignity and respect.
- Doing what you say you will do and doing it well.
- Being responsible and responsive.
- Being strong while being kind, humble, and proud.
- Open Minded.
- Being direct/brutally honest.
- I also brought to my endeavors practices I emphasized in the hotel industry:
- Great customer service.
- Attention to detail.
- Business best practice.
- Mental toughness and strength of will.

God blessed me with the ability to hold my focus under the screen of my mind to the exclusion of all outside distractions. I was also able to draw on my confidence, competence, and courage even more during my years of coaching, training, and professional development with the federal government focusing on Military Installation Management worldwide.

When the time came for me to plan my approach to the business, I brought all of my experience and insights to account, providing many professional services for my clients. I augmented my experience with two post-graduate advanced business degrees (MBA and MSc. Mgt) from the Graduate School of Management & Technology, University of Maryland College Park, MD; A Bachelor of Sciences degree in Organizational Management from Nyack College, Nyack, New York; and a graduate diploma of the U.S. Army's Premier Installation Management & Leadership Program from the Army Management Staff College (AMSC) Fort Belvoir, VA.

Considering my extensive education and experience, I was confident in my competence in providing the resources I offered my clients and doing so at a reasonable and fair price.

My next venture that's heavy on my mind is writing motivational/inspirational books. My purpose is to get others to do something, to inspire or challenge others' perspectives. And augment my book publishing with a podcast for small minority businesses. Let's see what happens…

CHAPTER 8

Formal Education, Training, and Professional Development

With my formal education, there was always a start somewhere. As mentioned in previous chapters, I came from a skilled trades environment—masonry and carpentry, and let's not forget farming—in Belgrade. Even if it were on a very small scale, we upheld the highest standards of professionalism.

Some of my brothers were employed at Mattocks' Masonry Company, LLC. They were all well trained, and they built beautiful residential homes and some commercial work all across the southeast region of the United States of America. They were experts at what they did and held high ethical standards. They were rarely, if ever, late for appointments, and you'd be hard-pressed to find a fault in their work. Most importantly, when they commit to a deadline, you can rely on timely delivery within their control.

None of my uncles, aunts, or any of the other elders in the generations before I graduated from elementary school. My cousin Adam, 12 years my senior, was my idol after graduating high school. He went off to college, graduated, and followed with an officer's commission in the Air Force. I wanted to be like him.

On the other hand, circumstances rerouted my parents, aunts, and uncles to a path where they could earn money so they'd be able to pay the bills and feed their families.

Through my experience, I can vouch for the fact that even though they were limited in academia, they were the most accomplished bunch when it came to common sense, commitment, and planned outcomes.

In other words, they proved that, without a doubt, you don't need a college degree to have common sense. They were smart, simple, honest, hardworking people. I submit that is why they were able to generate, though not necessarily high incomes, a sustaining business; they knew the secret to success lay in smart work, hard work, and determination.

Most of the income that kept the Mattocks families comfortable came from masonry, carpentry, and farming. The Mattocks family Klan had acres and acres of land, most of which were used for farming. Farming, like masonry and carpentry, was a success for the Mattocks families' farms.

All this common sense and smarts were in full practice while I was in primary through high school. However, with all this common sense and smartness, many of the family members concluded academia would be my best bet. They recognized early, as did I, that I wasn't meant for farming, masonry, or carpentry.

My enthusiasm for school was not only appreciated but encouraged, not only from within my immediate family but also from my aunts, uncles, and even others in the community. They all encouraged me to go out into the world and learn.

Belgrade wasn't the type of community that frowned on changing norms. They knew very well that the new and coming norms were different than tradition and that norms change with the times. And they always believed that education would always be needed for upward mobility. They believed I had what it took. Likewise, some of my cousins and others in my age bracket went off to college.

The only thing on everybody's mind was, "Go to school and focus on your learning," and I was committed to stepping up to that expectation. It was easy for me, and I felt I deserved it. I liked learning and increasing my knowledge. Hence, the culture of encouragement and appreciation, along with special care for those trying to improve themselves, became the cornerstone upon which I built my career.

As mentioned at the start of this book, my transition from a 19th-century three-room schoolhouse to a 20th-century full-fledged multi-building with multiple rooms and newly built bricks-and-blocks school was my springboard from traditional to new norms. Even though I was young, I took this as a blessing because I knew that it would give me more opportunities to learn and more exposure to others' perspectives. The school I was in before was a somewhat closed community, and even though that community was very good and promising, it didn't portray a realistic portrait of the world outside. For example, if there were twenty students and three different teachers in the classroom, chances were that eighteen of those students and all the teachers were likely to be aligned in their thought processes. That isn't necessarily how the world works. All children, including us from Belgrade, should be able to broaden our minds while learning to learn, apply, compare and contrast, synthesize, and maximize the use of what is, innovate when appropriate, and create when necessary. That learning would help us understand the true value and distinctions of facts, goals, approaches, and opinions. Insights into the aforementioned, I would submit, need to be learned/understood for them to be better able to protect themselves.

Even though the elementary school in Silverdale, North Carolina, was much bigger and provided many learning opportunities, it still had many similarities to the school I attended in Belgrade. More recently, I believe that schools have become more focused on being a money-making business than places of learning at the expense of minorities in general and blacks in particular. That was not the case back in my day. Back in Silverdale, the teachers, parents, and principals were aligned and focused on the students' learning. Those who didn't were brought up to speed and educated on the mission.

The school even took responsibility for the moral education of the children. Suppose a student fails to take responsibility for their assignments. In that case, you can bet that, unlike today, they would experience consequences, first by their teacher, then the principal, and then by their parents, who would always be informed. That might sound rough; after all, they were just kids. However, the elders weren't unfair. They were not unnecessarily harsh and didn't make any student think that they were in danger. They just had high expectations.

These days, it's hard to imagine being a child and having someone else show so much care toward your future and education. That's what teachers represented at Silverdale Elementary School, and I swear to this day that many other students would wholeheartedly agree with me.

That blessing got even bigger when I finished Silverdale Elementary and was promoted to Georgetown High School in Jacksonville, North Carolina. While I graduated four years later, in 1963, those blessings at Georgetown High were short-lived. As I mentioned earlier, you might recall that Georgetown High suffered a terrible fate three years following my graduation. It was subjected to an explosion and fire. However, before that, while I was learning there, I felt no difference in how I was being taught or in the teachers or the principal. Everything was consistent with Silverdale Elementary and Belgrade primary schools, except for the levels of challenges.

My learnings included treating people with respect, dignity, and self-sufficiency, and most importantly, I was informed on how to think, not what to think. The best thing about being in a huge high school was that I got to play sports. Yes, I was a "very" talented athlete back then and played baseball.

While the amusements and recreations in my life were fantastic, they were secondary to my learning. Mr. Broadhurst, the principal, made it clear to us students that no matter how good we were in sports, it would not be a substitute for education. It was such a strict rule that no one was allowed to play sports if their grades weren't up to par. Whenever I thought about higher education, it was rooted in my experiences in Belgrade, Silverdale, and Jacksonville and the lessons I needed to be self-sufficient to succeed in life.

When I finished high school, I was set to start college, and that's when everything turned upside down, starting with my head-on collision auto accident. Being told I was unlikely to ever walk again didn't sit well with my plans either. The most important thing in my life until that point had been a laser focus on education, as I believed that was my most promising way forward. There wasn't anyone who was going to help me. It was up to me alone, and the accident made it an even greater priority. The accident sidelined me for quite a few months, which gave me ample time to think while going through rehabilitation. One of the most important things that I thought about during that time was how I could study if I didn't have any money and couldn't work. Heck, I couldn't even walk.

But then, that old saying, "Where there's a will, there's a way," was planted like a seed in my innermost being, and I came up to be a living example of it. I found the will to get back up and walk again. No matter how many times I fell, I decided never, I mean never to give up in the face of adversity.

No, it didn't happen overnight, but it did happen, and it came as a surprise to all those who said, for example, it was futile even to try to walk. I didn't just walk; I ran. And, if I can properly recall, I did some cart-wheels too. Then I realized you don't walk alone in life. While dealing with my injury, some people were with me all the way. And then, some were just spectators as to how I was dealing with my injuries. In any case, I knew I must stay in control of myself, build good relationships with others, and keep calm, and I found it easier to deal with the challenges.

I couldn't delay my education any longer and was eager to go to school. Even though I was embarrassed to go to school with a slight limp and face some financial issues, I rejuvenated myself and was motivated to make it to a college campus. I just knew if I made it to that campus, I would be able to do the rest.

Eventually, with the "Where there's a will, there is a way" mindset, I regained full mobility and headed for Chicago, where I enrolled in the Chicago Institute of Technology (CIT). Over the next three semesters, I excelled in my studies. Everything was finally starting to fall into place. However, halfway through my fourth semester, CIT was facing credentials challenges. Worse, the credits I had earned were worthless since they couldn't be transferred. However, no one could take away what I had learned during those semesters. The only thing missing was an official transcript showing what courses I completed. The college hadn't issued it due to administrative issues.

While completely devastated, I decided that this was not an insurmountable roadblock. I knew the obstacles were only in my mind, and the less thought I gave them, the less they mattered. I knew the best thing to do was keep moving forward.

Whenever my resolve weakened a bit, I would ask myself,

"If I could come back from being told that I would never walk again to walking upright, without a limp, then how significant of a setback can this be?"

Sometimes we have to change our plans, so when I learned that the course credits received were not transferable, I decided that I was going to an environment where higher education wasn't required at the time. In a major stroke of luck—or maybe it was just fate—that's when I met my mentor in the hotel business, Peter Schruender. I had applied for a job as a bellhop at a fancy hotel, and Mr. Schruender quickly recognized me as management material and took me under his wing. From the bellhop, I went to the front desk, then the night-auditor, night shift manager, assistant manager, and General Manager. Throughout all of it, I never stopped learning.

I continued taking college classes and accumulated credits until I was able to earn my bachelor's degree in organization management from Nyack College in New York. After that, I continued taking courses at the University of Maryland University College.

At the time, I was working overseas for the military as a civilian. The blessing here was that the University of Maryland University College offered courses and programs everywhere I went, and I took every opportunity to take more courses earning two postgraduate degrees (MBA and MSc. Mgt.).

My pursuit of knowledge has never ended. I have always been in college, including summer executive classes. I learned the benefit of professional development as a trainer, advisor, and coach for the DoD (uniform and civilian) personnel for 25 years. I added all the skills learned from so many different walks of life that I was able to train and coach private and small businesses to become more forward thinkers.

I kept learning more because I was convinced that the day you stop learning is the day you stop growing. I am still learning, still teaching, which is one of the best learning experiences of all. Today, many people are amazed that I still have such a zest for life. Even though many people my age have retired, my zest for life and helping others keeps me going. There's no slowing down for me. I still feel very young at heart and young in my mind, young in the sense that I have a lot of energy and a lot to look forward to.

I spend my days, working with my wife, implementing new strategies and working toward our goals for our business and ourselves. I believe that, like wine, the mind gets better with age if you keep active. I know that the human brain is a very complex organ, with billions of neurons firing billions of electrical impulses each second. To that end, I refuse to let all that activity go to waste.

Many have so much life within them, but they don't take advantage of it because it might be outside their comfort zone. They may not realize they're missing out on wonderful experiences simply because they refuse to bear those moments of discomfort. To these individuals, I present myself as a living embodiment of the notion that small discomforts can lead to great rewards.

Seize the day!

www.ingramcontent.com/pod-product-compliance
Lightning Source LLC
Chambersburg PA
CBHW021655120626
46545CB00002B/868